ALL
ROAMS
LEAD
TO
RHODES

IAN
GRETTON

ALL
ROAMS
LEAD
TO
RHODES

Pensioners' progress through Greece

The Book Guild Ltd

First published in Great Britain in 2021 by
The Book Guild Ltd
9 Priory Business Park
Wistow Road, Kibworth
Leicestershire, LE8 0RX
Freephone: 0800 999 2982
www.bookguild.co.uk
Email: info@bookguild.co.uk
Twitter: @bookguild

Typeset in 11pt Minion Pro

Printed on FSC accredited paper
Printed and bound in Great Britain by 4edge Limited

ISBN 978 1913551 377

British Library Cataloguing in Publication Data.
A catalogue record for this book is available from the British Library.

To my sister Susan, who loved receiving my emails and encouraged me to do this.

INTRODUCTION

The morning bus from Stoupa to Kalamata climbs slowly up into the mountains, leaving the coastal village of Kardamyli far below and behind us. The road is narrow and ascends via a series of hairpin bends and short straights. As we near the summit, the point at which we will begin our descent towards the region's capital, an old man about three rows back shouts something to the driver, the traditional way of requesting a stop on a Greek bus. At the very summit, the driver pulls off the road into a passing place and stops the bus. The old man, who looks to be well into his eighties, stands unsteadily and with the aid of a stick totters hesitantly towards the front of the bus. We look around, astonished. We can see for miles in all directions and there isn't another road, a house or a farm in sight. Surely the driver isn't just going to abandon the old man? Or is someone else on their way to pick him up?

The entire bus holds its breath as the old man makes his faltering way down the three steep steps to the ground and disappears from our view. But the bus doesn't move off. We are aware of two young women across the aisle looking out of the window, then turning back, giggling, their hands over their mouths. Suddenly it becomes obvious to all. The old man is taking a pee against the side of the bus. After two or three minutes he climbs gingerly back up the steps and staggers back to his seat. The driver waits patiently until he's happy that the old man is comfortable, then pulls back onto the road and continues towards Kalamata.

PART ONE

The Cyclades

Part One

CHAPTER ONE

"The best meal in Athens"

It's lunchtime on a late April day as we emerge from the metro station at Syntagma Square, blinking in the bright sunlight. This square is the very heart of Athens and in recent months it has been the scene of emotional, often violent, demonstrations as ordinary Greeks continue to protest against their government's austerity measures. Greece is deep in debt, on the brink of bankruptcy, we've constantly been told, as the EU demands the repayment of billions of euros. But today there's no sign that this is the capital of a country that is allegedly on its knees. The square is busy, bustling, as hundreds of people, Athenians and tourists alike, go calmly and quietly about their business in the midday sunshine. They take no notice of us, two tired, grubby and slightly bewildered sixty-something Brits at the beginning of the fulfilment of a dream.

For years, Barbara has dreamed of retiring from work and travelling in Greece, seeing more of the country than we normally experience during package holidays spread over no more than a fortnight and spent in comfortable apartments in just one or two seaside villages. She finally retired from full-time work four months ago after more than twenty years at the University of Brighton. The following day we flew to Los Angeles, where her daughter Laura was then living and working, for a brief holiday. It was a bizarre Christmas that included watching an LA Lakers basketball game at the Staples Center (the fulfilment of one of *my* dreams!) and spending Christmas Day at a very crowded Disneyland, something I'd never really wanted to do but which I enjoyed enormously.

The time since we returned from California has been spent planning this trip. Or rather Barbara has been planning it. I've stood looking over her shoulder as she's worked the laptop, downloading bus timetables and ferry schedules, checking hotels, apartments and studios and arranging flights, and I've generally agreed with whatever she's suggested. With the benefit of many years visiting Greece, we want to do all our travelling on public transport and we're confident we know what's possible. We have some ferry crossings booked and the first couple of weeks' accommodation arranged. But after that we're basically winging it. The collection of guidebooks, maps and an iPad that are in our luggage should see us through. When we've told family and friends what we've been planning, they've described us as "OAP backpackers." Being well into our sixties, we're not sure our shoulders could carry the amount of luggage we need so we've plumped for more conventional suitcases on wheels instead. But the principle's the same. We've always thought of ourselves as travellers rather than tourists, and after two decades of visiting Greece on comfortable package holidays, where someone else has arranged the flights and accommodation, we're putting the theory to the test.

We stand for a minute or two, gazing around and getting used to the bright light and the heat, then wheel our bags the fifty metres or so to our hotel, the Arethusa, in the street called

Mitropoleos. It's a bland and modernised establishment, with rooms that are just about large enough for two people to spend the night. But it *is* very central. We change into clothes that are more suited to central Athens on a late spring afternoon than to Brighton's Pool Valley coach station at half-past three on a damp and chilly late spring morning and head out for some lunch – gyros and a cold beer for six euros a head. And then we wander back up to Syntagma Square and watch the evzones, the presidential guard, parading up and down outside the parliament building. They look ridiculous with their pom-pommed shoes and high-kicking *Monty Python* silly walk, even more so when a senior soldier in an ordinary uniform who's with them straightens their little skirts. But they're all about six feet four inches tall, and almost as much across the shoulders, so no one dares as much as titter.

We first came to Athens together in the winter of 2004, a few months before the city was due to host the Olympic Games, and were amazed to find that around almost every corner was an historic building, a Byzantine church or a fenced-off archaeological site. In the bright sunlight of a January day it looked very much as it does now, although we had noticed on our bus journey from the airport that the hills that partly surround the city were capped with snow. And when we went out in the evening, taverna owners in the Plaka, Athens's historic heart, would invite us to sit next to their roaring fire and share a warming raki with them.

When we go out for dinner a little later this evening, we don't need coats and we don't have to walk very far. Less than a hundred metres down Mitropoleos we turn into a narrow little side street called Patrou and are immediately entreated by a small man of about fifty to come and eat in his tiny hole-in-the-wall taverna called Aspro Alogo, or White Horse. I'm normally irritated by taverna touts and tend to walk away without even looking at their menus, but this guy, Marco, is particularly endearing. Rather than pleading with us he's inviting us politely, and we decide to go in. Well, not exactly 'in' but on the raised seating area outside where there are three or four tables and an assortment of kitchen chairs, few of them matching. Inside is a long, narrow room with another three or four tables down one side and the kitchen, where Marco's wife appears to prepare all the food on her own, on the other.

It's a long way from being the smartest place we've ever dined in and we wonder whether we've made the right choice – but not for long. It's a great example of not judging a book by its cover. The food is superb, the atmosphere friendly, and when we've finished Marco plies us, and everyone else presumably, with complimentary grapes, sweet dark coffee, raki and mastika. Our bill, which includes a half-litre of house red wine, comes to sixteen euros fifty, and as we leave Marco gives us each a half-litre bottle of water. Back in our room at the Arethusa, I Google Aspro Alogo out of curiosity and find a long list of effusive comments on TripAdvisor, more than one of which describes the food as the "best meal in Athens." I'm not sure it was *that* good, but it was what we hope will be the first of many memorable experiences.

We sink into our bed, exhausted but excited by the prospect of what lies ahead.

CHAPTER TWO

Milos – Aphrodite and Aborigines

It's late morning, and we check out of the Arethusa and haul our bags down the uneven pavements of Mitropoleos to Monastiraki Square, where we buy tickets for the metro train that will take us to the port of Piraeus.

The young man behind the grille in the ticket office looks at me suspiciously. "How old are you?" he asks.

I imagine he's seen our bulging bags and reckons we're too old for this sort of thing. "Sixty-nine," I reply, almost apologetically.

"That'll be sixty cents for you," the young man says with a smile. "It's half-price for seniors." Barbara has to pay the full fare, but it still only costs us one eighty for both of us to travel the twelve kilometres down to Piraeus. "And take care," the young man continues. "There are pickpockets on the train."

This first leg of our odyssey is taking us to the Cyclades, the island group that gets its name from the fact that it roughly circles the so-called sacred isle of Delos, which we aim to visit in about three weeks' time, and it is at Piraeus where we need to get our first ferry. When we were here in January 2004, we made the same metro journey from the city centre. On a bright, cold afternoon, we stood on the harbour where much of Jules Dassin's 1960 classic movie *Never on Sunday* had been filmed, looking at the ferries and wishing we could just board one of them and head off to one of the islands. Well now we're going to. But not immediately. One of those typical turns of Greek logic allows us to collect our pre-booked tickets for next Monday morning's ferry from Milos to Folegandros but not those for the 16.30 from Piraeus to Milos this afternoon (also pre-booked) – not until half past two anyway. We settle down outside a quayside taverna and enjoy a leisurely beer and then lunch.

We've pre-booked the ferry because tomorrow's a bank holiday, May Day, and given that it will be a Friday Athenians are likely to be escaping the city in their thousands to enjoy a long weekend on the islands. It's also the worldwide workers' holiday, and, bearing in mind the ongoing problems in Greece, an excellent opportunity to demonstrate. Unless you enjoy tear gas and police batons, central Athens probably won't be a great place to be. So we collect our tickets and board the Aegean Speed Lines ferry *Speedrunner 4* en route to Milos via Serifos and Sifnos, as early as possible, ensuring that we can choose a seat. *Speedrunner 4* is huge, spacious and comfortable but rapidly fills up, and before long we find ourselves sitting with Otto and Charlotte from New Hampshire, a rosy-cheeked healthy-looking couple who're probably in their late forties and who "just love talking to other folks."

In fairness, it's a more than pleasant way of passing the time. Otto and Charlotte also love travelling and the outdoor life and are fulfilling *their* lifelong ambition to visit Greece. They hired a car at Athens airport when they arrived yesterday, drove it into the city centre and have now left it there, safe in a hotel car park, while they spend a few days visiting one or two islands. We're also joined by a young half-Greek/half-Scottish man called

Nicholas, and his fiancée, who shares his delicious sesame seed and honey biscuits with us and advises Otto and Charlotte not to go into any restaurants that have pictures of the food displayed outside. (If we'd taken that advice, we wouldn't have gone into Aspro Alogo last night, or any number of other wonderful tavernas we've enjoyed over the years, but we don't say so.) Sadly, all four of our new friends leave the ferry at Serifos at seven, as do dozens of other passengers, and we're left on our own for the remainder of the journey.

It's eight forty-five and dark by the time we dock at Adamas, the little port town of Milos, founded by Cretan refugees in the 1830s and regarded as the safest natural harbour in the Aegean. Back at home, Barbara has had an email conversation with Petros, the owner of the Dionysis Studios where we're staying for the next four nights, and he's promised to meet us off the ferry holding up a board with her name on it. We wheel our bags down the ship's ramp and wait on the quayside. And wait. And wait. *Speedrunner 4* disgorges its passengers and vehicles, reloads and heads off to Kythnos and we stand there on our own, looking in vain for Petros and his board. Taxis come and go. Drivers ask where we're going and if they can take us there. We keep refusing until, eventually, Barbara phones Petros. He's having trouble with his car, he tells us. He's been watching the television rather than the time and didn't realise the ferry had arrived, but he'll be with us in two or three minutes.

This time, however, he's as good as his word. Within less than five minutes we are being approached by a short, generously moustachioed man of about sixty who introduces himself as Petros, shakes our hands enthusiastically then marches us a couple of hundred metres to the Dionysis building. As we walk through the busy little square at the centre of the town he points out a couple of banks and tells us we can use their ATMs.

"Will there be any money in them?" I ask, less than half-seriously. Because of what we've been hearing and reading at home about Greek banks being constantly short of cash and about to run out at any time, we've tucked fifteen hundred euros in cash, far more than we'd normally carry, into the linings of our bags just in case they do run dry.

Petros laughs. "You don't want to believe all that German propaganda," he says. "Everything's fine. There's no problem." Yanis Varoufakis, the charismatic former Finance Minister, has confidently declared that the EU won't allow Greece to go bankrupt. If the country is forced to leave the euro, he says, the common currency will collapse. Petros seems happy with that.

It's already turned nine o'clock and the shops are mostly shut – and mostly won't be open tomorrow. We go out almost immediately after dumping our luggage in the apartment, managing to find the one minimarket that is still open. We buy food for tomorrow's breakfast, as well as a litre of wine and a bottle of Metaxa – we have to have the essentials – and then settle down at a nearby taverna. It's still busy at eleven when we leave, more than happy after excellent gyros and a complimentary half-litre of house red wine, delivered by a waiter who apologises for the slow service and then brings us a bill for fifteen-fifty. We like Milos already.

*

The sun streams in at our window and by seven-thirty it's hot on our east-facing balcony. About fifty metres directly behind the studio, across a stretch of scrubby derelict land, there's a small modern supermarket, shuttered and showing no signs of opening. After we've had breakfast Petros invites us into his office and gives us a verbal guided tour of the island, using a knitting needle to point out places of interest on a map he has Blu-Tacked to the wall. Milos is the most westerly of the Cyclades and as steeped in history and Hellenic culture as the rest of the archipelago. But sadly, today's a public holiday, everywhere's closed and there aren't any buses. The taxi drivers are also likely to be taking the day off, so we'll have to make do with what Adamas itself has to offer.

Which isn't a massive amount, but on this beautiful morning, just the second full day of our expedition, we're happy just to stroll around, visiting churches – most of which *are* open – taking photographs and getting the feel of the Cyclades again. We first came to these islands in 2007, basing ourselves in Parikia, on Paros, and visiting several of the other islands, and, once we'd become used to the almost constant wind, we fell in love with them. At lunchtime today, we're invited into the kitchen at Trapatselis, the taverna where we've chosen to eat, to see what's been freshly cooked. The young man looking after us tells us it's going to be twenty-six or twenty-seven degrees (Celsius) for the next four or five days, even with the strong wind. It's better than usual for this time of year, he says, and it comes after a worse-than-usual winter when he says it snowed on Milos on at least three occasions.

Snow on a Greek island seems a little more credible in the evening, when it's noticeably cooler and the tavernas around the harbour have rolled down the transparent plastic screens that shelter the diners and drinkers from the wind. People are out in their numbers now, enjoying the first evening of the holiday weekend, and we go to the highly recommended Flisvos fish taverna. We shouldn't do it because the average ten-year-old Greek child speaks English to a standard that I'll never be able to achieve in Greek, but a favourite pastime wherever we go in the world is spotting amusing translations on menus and elsewhere. In Greece you can barely find a restaurant that doesn't serve "lamp", generally "lamp in the oven" or "lamp chops", but Flisvos sets the bar so high that it's unlikely to be surpassed on this trip with its "Kleftiko pork with cheese and Aborigines". We don't try it, but the food we do have is excellent.

The following morning it seems that our lunchtime waiter's weather forecast is proving correct. It's warm, there's a clear, cloudless sky and the wind isn't quite as strong as yesterday. It's still there, but not quite as strong. We've lost our wi-fi signal and there's another aspect of life at Dionysis that's puzzling us. Petros has posted notices all over the building saying "Please save water" and pointing out that natural resources are precious on this small island. He's not alone among Greek landlords in seemingly failing to realise that one of the best ways of saving water would be to have plugs in all the sinks and washbasins. Or at least some of them.

It's Saturday and life on Milos has returned to normal. The little modern supermarket behind Dionysis is already showing signs of life. The shutters have been raised, the boxes of fresh fruit and vegetables stacked outside, the day's special offers magic-marked on a white board. In the little square we take the ten-thirty bus to Plaka, officially the island's capital four kilometres away at the top of a hill. A short walk of about half a kilometre down a road and about the same distance down a steep flight of steps later we reach the Catacombs, said to be one of the best-preserved early Christian monuments in Greece.

We pay our three euros each for a guided tour of this spooky subterranean burial ground, which was only excavated and restored between 2007 and 2009. The Catacombs date from the first century AD and when first discovered they were still full of bones. But contact with fresh air quickly reduced the bones to dust, and apart from the niches where the bodies were laid to rest all that remains are a few inscriptions in red and some more recent black graffiti. And then, emerging into the sunlight again, we wander along a little narrow path until we reach a small, almost hidden sign indicating that it was here that one of the world's most famous works of art was discovered.

It was in 1820 that a local farmer ploughing the hillside dug up a marble sculpture alleged to be that of Aphrodite, the Greek goddess of love. Through the same kind of dubious trading that saw the Elgin Marbles end up in the British Museum, the sculpture found its way to the Louvre in Paris. The Aphrodite of Milos was unveiled at the Louvre in 1821 and has since been seen by the many millions of visitors to the museum who know it as the Venus de Milo. Like many of Greece's archaeological sites, the spot where this amazing discovery was made is overgrown and uncared for, marked only by the shabby fading blue and yellow sign proclaiming "Site of the discovery of Venus of Milos" in Greek and English, but the view over the little seaside village of Klima and the well-preserved Roman amphitheatre and across the flooded volcanic caldera towards Agios Dimitriou on the island's north-western tip is stunning.

Not far away, another significant piece of historic art was found at around the same time, the head of what would have been a colossal marble statue depicting the god Asclepius. The Asclepius of Milos, as it inevitably became known, was 'acquired' in 1867 by the British Museum, where it remains on show to this day.

There's a growing amount of cloud as we walk back up to the centre of Plaka to get the bus back to Adamas. We sit down on the terrace of a taverna called En Plo and order two beers. The owner brings us our drinks, as well as a plate of delicious olives, tomatoes, capers and cucumber that almost counts as lunch, and asks where we're from. And then he proceeds to reel off a list of places in England that he's visited – Southampton, Plymouth, Bristol, Hull and so on, all port cities so we assume he must at one time have been a seaman. No doubt he'll tell us he had a girl in each of the places he's named if we ask.

It's cloudy, breezy and cool this evening, and behind the plastic screens at Marianna, an excellent waterfront taverna, the brothers who seem to run it offer another free half-litre of house red wine. No explanation given this time, it's just Greek hospitality. Patrick Leigh Fermor wrote in his book on the Mani that in Ancient Greece the words for 'stranger' and 'guest' were the same, which explains much about the modern-day attitude towards visitors. The brothers tell us that eighty per cent of their customers over the past few days have been English, although we think it may just be that eighty per cent of their customers have been *speaking* English. We haven't come across any fellow Brits in three days on this island. A lot of French, who smoke constantly and make the closed-in tavernas slightly less comfortable than were they to be in the open, some Scandinavians and Germans, but no Brits.

CHAPTER THREE

Folegandros – "Sorry, I'm in Athens"

As we're leaving Dionysis Studios on Monday morning to walk to the port and get the ferry to Folegrandros, Petros calls us into his office again. He opens a drawer in his desk and takes out a small balsa-wood model sailing boat, about six inches tall and brightly painted in the Greek colours of blue and white, and offers it to us.

"A little gift for you to remember Milos," he says. We thank him profusely, resist the temptation to suggest that he buys some plugs for his sinks and washbasins, shake his hand and say our goodbyes. The little boat is fragile and it will be quite an achievement if it gets back to Brighton in one piece.

This is where our journey really begins. This ferry and our accommodation on Folegrandros are the last things we have pre-booked in the Cyclades. We really are winging it through the archipelago from here on. Folegandros is one of the places we're visiting that I'd never heard of before we started planning this trip. I just stood behind Barbara at the laptop and when she said, "Folegandros looks nice," I agreed. Judging by the online photographs, it was going to be beautiful – and now we're on our way. It's in the southern Cyclades and, with fewer than six hundred inhabitants, one of the smallest islands in Greece that have a permanent population. Our guidebook describes it as "bleak, arid and mountainous," which doesn't sound terribly promising, but it also suggests that there are "sheer cliffs and breathtaking scenery," which should compensate for any alleged bleakness and aridity.

It's a very small island, no more than twelve kilometres by four, with a dark past as a place of exile for political prisoners from Roman times to the military dictatorship of 1967–74. The former Socialist prime minister George Papandreou was among the island's reluctant visitors. In 2005 an American travel magazine described Folegandros as "Greece's most beautiful undiscovered island," which ought to have opened the tourism floodgates. But because of its remoteness and the lack of reliable ferry connections with centres like Athens, it didn't. It has, we understand, remained relatively undisturbed.

The nine-twenty ferry from Milos to Folegandros actually leaves closer to ten-thirty, but none of the handful of passengers waiting seems to mind the delay. They're more concerned about getting the precise seats whose numbers appear on their tickets, even though the vessel is no more than half-full. One thing you learn very early when travelling independently in Greece is how fussy the locals can be about where they sit on public transport. If you're a tourist, you should never sit in the front seats of an empty Greek bus, for instance. At the next stop after you've sat down an elderly Greek will almost certainly board the bus and stare at you until you feel you have no option but to get up and move further back so they can sit at the front. When the buses are busier, each time someone sitting near the front gets off, others will move down the bus to take over the newly vacated seats until they eventually reach the very front – where they will remain for two or three stops until they alight.

It's little more than an hour until the high-speed ferry pulls into the little harbour at Karovastasis (pop. fifty-five), where Theo, a friend of our landlord here, is waiting to drive us the short distance around the bay to our accommodation at Coral Apartments. It's a smart, relatively new complex, several blocks of two or three apartments each set in spacious grounds – and we appear to be the only people staying there at the moment. Our apartment is large and well-furnished with two balconies that have stunning views across the bay and as far as Santorini, but no working wi-fi at the moment and no electric kettle.

When we first started coming to Greece together in the 1990s nowhere provided a kettle, but in recent years we've grown used to having one as holiday property owners have come to realise it's what their Northern European guests expect. But not on Folegandros yet, it would appear. Never mind, we'll boil the water for our morning tea in one of the saucepans. When we stayed in Kalyves, on Crete, a few years ago the apartment also didn't have a kettle. We'd put the water in a pan, put it on one of the hot plates and turn the dial up to maximum. And then there would be a loud bang as the apartment's master fuse blew and all the lights went out and our iPod stopped playing. We reported it to Christos, the landlord who lived downstairs, who eventually came up to the apartment to see for himself. He turned the dial up to maximum – bang! He tried it again – same result.

"Don't turn it up so high," he said with a shrug, and left us. That worked, obviously, but it took half an hour to boil the water every time we wanted a cup of tea. Here in Folegandros all we have in the kitchen area is a large fridge-freezer and a two-ringed hob, but at least using the hob doesn't blow the fuses and we can enjoy a cup of tea while we unpack.

Clustered around the pretty fishing harbour are a few houses, two or three tavernas, of which only one is open, and a minimarket, which while appearing to be well-stocked is also shut. We sit down outside the open taverna, Kalymnios, and eventually the young woman who runs it appears. Given the levels of stock we can see through the windows, we assume the shop next door has just closed for lunch. "Do you know when it opens again?" we ask the woman, gesturing in the direction of the minimarket.

She disappears into the taverna for a few moments, then reappears. "About ten days," she says, matter-of-factly. But she does serve us a really good Greek salad and some excellent fresh calamari and we're finished in time to get the island bus up to the island's main town, Chora, where, hopefully, something *will* be open.

Actually, 'bus' is flattering the vehicle somewhat. It's a boneshaking, rattling twelve-seat minibus of questionable vintage painted in the blue and white stripes of the Greek flag and driven by a deeply tanned sixty-ish Greek who will become a familiar face and almost a friend over the next few days. It shudders up the hilly, winding road and at times makes us wonder whether we're going to get to our destination, or even around the next bend, but eventually we do and we are treated to some amazing views over the bluest, clearest sea imaginable. The ride is worth the discomfort.

The main settlement on almost all small Greek islands is called Chora. It literally means 'town', it will have a population of anything from a few dozen to a few hundred (in Folegandros's case five hundred and thirteen) and while it may have an alternative, more imaginative, name 'Chora' is what appears on the maps and road signs. There are variations, such as Megalochora (large town), Paleochora (old town) and Neochora (new town), but here we are in the narrow streets and alleyways of plain old Chora. Not that there is anything remotely plain about it. It's a beautiful, typically Greek village perched on a ridge of invasion-proof cliffs that rise almost vertically up over three hundred metres from the sea. It's quiet, because cars are banned from the centre, a blaze of colour from window boxes and large pots of bougainvillea and hibiscus outside front doors and oozing Greek islands charm. It's said to be one of the best preserved and most dramatically sited *choras* in the Aegean, an assertion with which at this moment it's difficult to argue.

In one of the small streets we find the Folegandros travel office. It's one of the few places that's open at the moment, so we go in and discuss with the young woman behind the counter where we might travel to next. Eventually, we plump for Paros, an island we know and have been looking forward to revisiting. There's a ferry from Folegandros to Naxos on Thursday morning and we know that it's an easy hop from there because we've done it before. The problem is that our reservations can't be confirmed because there's no internet connection at the moment – just as there wasn't down in Karovastasis – so we'll have to come back. We leave a deposit and seek out a minimarket for some essential supplies.

Back down at the patch of waste ground on the edge of the village that's amusingly described as the Bus Station, there's a handwritten timetable Blu-Tacked to a wall. It's now about two-thirty in the afternoon and the next bus back to Karovastasis isn't for another four hours. Who moves around at this time of day? Why on earth would you need buses? Next to the timetable there's a little poster advertising the island's taxi service, so, not wanting to sit around for four hours, we decide to call the mobile number provided. It rings for a while before a man's voice answers.

"Do you speak English?" we ask in our most respectful tone.

"Of course," the man answers brightly.

"We'd like a taxi to take us from Chora to Karovastasis, please."

"When?"

"Well, now. Or as soon as possible anyway."

"I'm sorry, I can't come at the moment."

"How long then?" We're in no great hurry. We can probably find a taverna, sit and have a drink or two while we're waiting.

There's a slight pause, and then, "Two days. Maybe three."

"Two *days*?"

"Yes. I'm in Athens having the car repaired. It will be Wednesday or Thursday before I come back." Maybe he owns the minimarket in Karovastasis as well.

"Is there another taxi on the island?"

"Sorry, no." The line goes dead.

We have two choices. We can sit outside a taverna all afternoon until it's time for the bus – very tempting – or we can walk. It's no more than four kilometres and it's all downhill, but even at the beginning of May the temperature's already in the high twenties and there's unlikely to be any shade. But in the end we choose the Mad Dogs and English OAPs option anyway and set off on foot.

It proves to be much less arduous than we'd feared. Spurred on by the prospect of downing one of the cold beers that are clinking away in my little rucksack before they get too warm, we find a pace that suits us and make our way along the side of a road that twists and turns gently downwards through the barren landscape. It seems less steep when you're going down on foot than it did when ascending in the bus. Occasionally a car or flat-bed truck passes but, despite what we hope, no one stops to offer us a lift and it's beneath our dignity to attempt to flag someone down. In the sunlight, the sandy soil and the occasional patches of red and yellow flowers give the impression that we're walking across the surface of a giant orange. It's hot and, as we'd feared, there is no shade, but we eventually make it. The journey actually takes less than an hour, and when we arrive at the Coral Apartments we find the wi-fi has been restored. We open a bottle of Mythos, get out the iPad and crack on with the task of finding some accommodation on Paros.

Dinner at Kalymnios, an establishment which the tour manager of one of our American road trips would have described as "the only game in town", is at thirty-five euros the most expensive we've had since we left Brighton, and likely to be one of the most expensive we'll have in Greece, at least until we get to Mykonos. But this is a small and relatively inaccessible island. It was never going to be cheap, not by Greek standards anyway, and maybe that's the price of being this close to paradise. It's a beautiful evening and we're seated outside the taverna watching the sun set behind the hills that almost completely surround the bay. To our right, pleasure boats – small dinghies with outboard motors, larger yachts – sit dead still on the calm water. To our left, at the jetty where the ferries arrive, a handful of fishing boats are moored, some burning lights as their owners repair and prepare nets for their next expedition. The wind has dropped, and apart from the chink of cutlery on plates at the two or three other tables that are occupied and the gentle lapping of the sea on the beach, there's barely a sound.

*

The following morning we're both awake by seven, which is odd and slightly annoying because it's still as silent as it was last evening, one of the quietest places we've ever been. The only sound is that of birds – pigeons, sparrows, the odd cock crowing somewhere in the distance – and the mournful-sounding bleating of a goat somewhere in the surrounding hills. Maybe it has an idea that it's very shortly destined for a large cooking pot with some delicious lemon sauce. At nine, Ioanna, the young housekeeper here at Coral, is outside on her hands and knees, painting thick bright white lines on the cracks in the crazy paving, Cyclades-style. She's not the only person around with a paint brush in hand. Almost everywhere seems to be getting a fresh white coat for the impending summer season.

The peace is shattered at ten by the announcement of the arrival of the car ferry *Korais*, which gives us a demonstration of the fast turnarounds for which Greek ferries are renowned. It's truly remarkable how quickly they manage to unload and reload – which raises the question, "Why do Greek ferries never seem to run on time?" The 11am bus to Chora doesn't actually leave Karovastasis until eleven-thirty – because this morning's *SeaJet2* is running almost half an hour late and our driver has to wait for it. But we still have time to revisit the travel agency and collect our tickets for the Naxos ferry, explore a little more of the pretty island capital, have a leisurely beer outside a taverna, buy some groceries and get the half past one bus back to Karovastasis, which *does* run on time.

Back down at sea level it's as quiet as ever – apart from the bleating goat who for the moment seems to have secured a reprieve. He may have been given a stay of execution, but the island's rabbit population hasn't been so lucky. "Local rabbit" is the special on the menu at Kalymnios on our last evening on Folegandros, bad news for fans of *Watership Down* but good news for people like me who love rabbit and get too few opportunities to enjoy it back at home. It's a treat we reckon we've earned, having walked down from Chora again this afternoon. In fact, there isn't a great deal else to do on the island other than walking – apart from eating, drinking and generally relaxing, of course – but it is the perfect place for just that. Dozens of well-worn tracks criss-cross the landscape, it's hilly but not too strenuous, although there is precious little shelter from the sun, but the views are to die for. Oh, and the rabbit was delicious.

Chapter Four

Paros – "If you miss the boat you lose the ticket"

SeatJet2 has barely left the harbour on Folegandros when we're approached by a young Greek woman in a smart white shirt and dark grey pencil skirt.

"You are travelling to Naxos?" she asks, although it's almost as much of a statement as a question. We reply that we are.

"You must come with me at Ios," she continues. "This vessel doesn't go to Naxos anymore. We will wait at Ios for another ferry that does." No explanation is given for the change in the itinerary.

It's a nuisance, since we'd envisaged settling down for a couple of hours, catching up on some reading and not having to haul our luggage off and on ferries halfway through the crossing. But on the plus side, it will be an island grab that we hadn't planned. We follow orders without question.

Ios is a notorious party island, nicknamed the Benidorm of the Aegean, but apparently desperate these days to change its image, with what are said to be the best beaches in the Cyclades. But we don't have time to find out. We stand on the quayside at Ormos, the main port, for no more than twenty minutes or so before the *Masterjet* comes along, almost twice the size of *SeaJet2* but with about half the number of passengers. We store our bags on the level at which we board and settle down in the upper lounge with a beer and a sandwich, and within just over an hour we're disembarking at Naxos. The largest island in the Cyclades, we were on Naxos briefly in 2007, although we didn't travel far from the seafront. Since we'll be moving on later today, we don't intend to do much different this time, although we'll almost certainly be back on the island soon since it's something of a hub. We find the ferry office near the port and buy our tickets for the six o'clock crossing to Paros, leave our bags in left luggage and head off for some lunch.

It doesn't take long to find somewhere we fancy. Naxos town has a tightly packed line of tavernas and bars along a kilometre-long stretch of the waterfront, many of them with tables that look out across the eight-kilometre strait that separates the island from Paros. Among them is Smyrneiko, where we order first a beer and then some lunch. As he brings us the almost obligatory free ouzo at the end of the meal, the owner asks us where we're from.

"I went to London once," he tells us in the most perfect English we've heard for almost a fortnight. "I sang at the Albert Hall."

We're impressed. "You're a singer?"

"There were twenty-seven of us in the choir," he replies. "It was 1984, we were very young. I don't remember much about it now." He doesn't elaborate and disappears back into the kitchen.

Blue Star Line's *Delos*, a massive roll-on roll-off car ferry, sets a new standard in late-running for our travels so far, leaving Naxos almost an hour after its scheduled departure time. But it's comfortable, with plenty of seating available, and it takes little more than an hour to cross the strait to Paros. We've sailed into the main port Parikia on several previous occasions, always a little apprehensively. There are some nasty-looking rocky outcrops at the entrance to the bay, and one evening in 2000 a similar vessel to the *Delos* struck some of these rocks and sank – and eighty-one passengers and crew perished. At the subsequent inquiry it was revealed that the captain and first officer had put the ship on autopilot so they could watch a football match on television. The first officer was jailed for nineteen years for manslaughter, the captain received sixteen. Two senior managers of the ferry company committed suicide between the sinking and the inquiry.

Happily, there have been no similar mishaps since. And now, down on the car deck the huge rear door of the ship is lowered open to the stirring accompaniment of 'Ride of the Valkyries' blasting out over the PA system and cars, trucks, bikes and foot passengers surge forward up the ramp and onto the quayside. There's a disused windmill in the centre of a roundabout as you leave the port, and just as in 2007 it's surrounded by absolute chaos. Added to the traffic leaving the ferry are the buses that all seem to leave the adjoining bus station at the same time, taxis cruising on the lookout for fares and cars, coaches, bikes and trucks, as well as foot passengers, surging in the opposite direction to board the ferry.

We're approached several times and asked if we want a room, a taxi or a hire car. We don't. Mina, our landlady here, has texted and agreed to meet us and drive us to our accommodation, but in the maelstrom there's little hope of spotting her. We stand by the roundabout and wait patiently until the traffic has subsided, the backpackers have gone and we're virtually the only people left. Eventually, with the aid of further text messages, Mina and I identify each other and we cross the road to exchange greetings. She leads us away from the port and we walk for about five hundred metres before Mina stops in a side street next to a white Transit van bearing the name of the family door and replacement window business. She crams our bags into the back among the white PVC doors and windows, then we squeeze into the van's front seats. We drive for another five hundred metres before Mina pulls up outside the smart new apartment block called Panos, our home for the next four days. She checks our passports to confirm that we are who we claim to be, then lets us choose which room we'd like to stay in from several that are unoccupied.

*

We loved Paros, and particularly Parikia, when we were here ten years ago. Barbara's daughter Sarah and her then boyfriend James found it so romantic when they came here the following year that they returned home engaged to be married. (The wedding was a year later.) Despite the fact that it has become enormously popular with holidaymakers in recent years, the islanders have managed to maintain an authentic Greek island atmosphere. Paros probably has less to offer in the way of history and culture than many of its neighbours, but it's a beautiful place. And it is the source of Parian marble, arguably the finest in the world and used by sculptors since Classical times. Some of the great masterpieces of Ancient Greek sculpture, as well as the tiles on the roof of the Parthenon in Athens, have used Parian marble.

One of our favourite ways of passing the time on our previous visit here was to buy a beer just before midday and sit outside a bar opposite the ferry port. We would then watch the mayhem unfold as two or three large ferries came in almost at the same time. The confusion would be compounded by the three buses to various parts of the island all leaving the bus station at twelve-twenty. In idle moments after we returned home I would log on to the Paros webcam, which is fixed high above the windmill roundabout, and watch it all happen again, same scenario day after day.

Increasingly these days, Greek studios and apartments have televisions. And almost without exception, you can only find Greek TV stations on them. So once we're properly awake this morning we find BBC1 on the iPad and watch live coverage of the UK general election (we've postal-voted). It's only about 5.30am UK time so the results are still coming in. Theresa May has called an early election so that she can establish a "strong and stable" Conservative government. It's looking like one of the worst errors of judgement in politics for some time, as the Conservative majority David Cameron won two years ago is being wiped out. At least Caroline Lucas, our Green MP in Brighton Pavilion, has been re-elected with an increased majority.

After the excitement of the election, I sit on the balcony and finish reading Paul Theroux's *Dark Star Safari*, his account of the journey he made from Cairo to Cape Town in the year that he turned sixty. It's the kind of adventure that makes what we're now doing seem like a gentle stroll in the park.

What there is of archaeological and historical interest in Parikia can probably be covered in a morning's stroll around the town. About fifty metres from our front door is what we assume to be the "Open-air Sanctuary." We only know that because of the signs that direct us towards it. But there are no information boards, access to the remains is, predictably, overgrown and the site itself is tucked away in an unremarkable little corner. Not far away are two more sites, both about the size of a tennis court and side by side. A sign tells us that one is a "Hellenistic Mosaic", the other is a "Mosaic of the Hellenistic Period". That's all the information we have, so we'll never know the difference between them. When you have as many ancient and sacred sites as the Greeks do, you can probably afford to be casual about them. Unearth the remains, clean them up, stick a brown and yellow sign on the site – and then leave them. That seems to be the Greek way.

The Ekatontapyliani, or 'Church of a Hundred Doors', is, on the other hand, far from neglected. A sixth-century Byzantine church that has been substantially restored over the years, it's said that ninety-nine entrances, some so small that only a mouse can squeeze through, have been found. When the one-hundredth door is discovered, according to some stories, Constantinople will be returned to the Greeks. There's more restoration work going on at the moment, and the wooden scaffolding reaching up inside the dome makes it look much like it might have done when it was originally being built fifteen hundred years ago. But even if today's builders and restorers do find the one-hundredth mousehole, it seems unlikely, given the long-standing antipathy between Greece and Turkey, that Istanbul will become a Greek enclave.

*

The mountainous little island of Antiparos lies about two kilometres off the south-west coast of Paros. It is, according to our guidebook, the "octopus capital of Greece," and it's suggested that these eight-legged creatures may have some hitherto undiscovered aphrodisiac qualities since on Antiparos, unlike anywhere else in the Cyclades, the resident population is increasing year-on-year. But when we set off after breakfast it's not in search of an octopus lunch but the island's best-known attraction, The Cave.

We take the bus down the coast to Pounda and the car ferry for the brief crossing to Antiparos's main settlement – that's either Chora (of course) or Kastro, whichever sign you happen to be looking at but which has a wide street linking the port to a pretty square lined with tavernas and bars. Waiting near the square is a small fleet of coaches that transport tourists the eight kilometres into the hills to one of the Cyclades's most remarkable natural phenomena. A massive stalagmite, said to be forty-five million years old and the largest in Europe, guards the entrance to the cave and four hundred steps take you down into the spooky one-hundred-metre-deep chamber. I have to admit that it is so steep and difficult in places that we lose our bottle and don't make it all the way down, just far enough to be awed.

Nor are we tempted to break off bits of stalactite and take them home as souvenirs, as famous names such as Lord Byron and the nineteenth-century King Otto of Greece are said to have done. But at least they and dozens of others carved or smoked their names on the walls to make up for it, turning the place into a sort of giant subterranean autograph book. One stalactite even bears witness (in Latin) to the fact that a candlelit mass was celebrated there on Christmas Day 1673, led by the French Ambassador and attended by five hundred locals. Despite the wobbly knees and a hint of vertigo, it's a wonderful experience.

We take the fast ferry back to Parikia and settle down for a late lunch at Christos, a small taverna opposite the port, and are not only fed well but entertained by a waiter who has that wonderful gift of being able to tell jokes in a language other than his mother-tongue. When he brings us our half-litre jug of house red wine we ask for a bottle of water. "You won't need any," he answers, a deadpan expression on his face. "I've already put some in the wine."

Shortly afterwards, he leaves the taverna, hops onto his moped and disappears. He returns about twenty minutes later and tells us, "I've just been for something to eat. I don't like the food here!"

*

This morning we sit on our sun-trapped, sheltered-from-the-Cycladean-wind balcony, reading and watching everyday Parikian life unfold. Mina's father is working on the little plot of dusty land where he keeps a few chickens and grows vegetables. An elderly woman in black on her way home from the shops crosses herself multiple times as she passes the little church opposite Panos Studios. Two scrawny cows, their tails vigorously swatting away insects, graze in a scrubby field. Beyond the neighbouring buildings and the trees that help deaden the noise, trucks thunder their way towards the port. Life goes on, unaffected by occasional visitors like us.

We wander along to the port and peruse the ferry timetables in a travel agent's office, eventually booking tickets for the crossing to Iraklia in two days' time. I've never heard of the island before (another one!), but if we're going to get there we'll need to be at the port in good time. At the foot passenger entrance a sign warns us "Passengers are obliged to be at the port thirty minutes before departure... In case you miss the boat you lose the ticket." And after we've got our tickets we catch the bus to Naoussa, in the north of the island. Once one of the most important ports in the Cyclades, Naoussa is now smart, trendy and self-conscious, a lovely fishing village that has become something of a jet set hang-out. It's very white and very clean and the on-street parking spaces are full of Mercedes and BMWs, all of them with Greek registration plates. It's windy and the tavernas that line the narrow beach have their protective plastic sheets down. Taverna Glafkos serves excellent food, even if Nikitas the owner has felt the need to 'westernise' his dishes.

We get the same feeling about Albatross, a large taverna in the port area of Parikia where we go for dinner, but, apart from these minor aberrations, Paros hasn't disappointed. But after four days doing very little, it's time to move on again.

CHAPTER FIVE

Iraklia – Snakes in the grass

Nel Lines' *Aqua Spirit*, due to leave Parikia at 08.55, is only about twenty minutes behind schedule. Having been warned by the notice that we dare not be late, we have a minor panic when Mina, who has promised to drive us down to the port, doesn't turn up when she said she would. In the end, we give up waiting and set off at a brisk pace, hauling our luggage behind us, and make it to the departure gate seconds before the thirty-minute deadline. We needn't have worried – predictably, we're almost the first in the queue. A Scandinavian family – mum, dad and two children aged about ten and eight, all with massive rucksacks – have also heeded the warning and are the only other people already there. The remaining passengers, Greeks, are still turning up as the ferry is loading.

Aqua Spirit, heading for Iraklia via Naxos, is old, a little rusty and tired-looking on the outside, but it has clearly had a refit and it's smart and comfortable on the inside and, on the first leg of the journey, not very busy. We go up to the lounge, buy a coffee and settle down with our books. The first thing that greets us as we enter the bay at Agios Giorgos, the little port of Iraklia, after the three-hour journey is what looks like a small North Sea oil platform but is in fact a unique example of modern technology. Installed in 2007 by the University of the Aegean, it's the world's first floating seawater desalination plant. Quite how effective it has proved is debatable, and, despite the publicity it has received, no one we speak to over the next few days is sure if it's even working any more. The largest in area of the islands known as the Lesser Cyclades, Iraklia, resident population a hundred and fifty-one, has no natural water supply and at the moment still has all its fresh water shipped in by tanker. This group of tiny islands of which Iraklia is the largest is also known as the Back Islands, allegedly because most Greeks regard them as the back of beyond.

We arrive in Agios Georgios, the port village that is no more than a scattered handful of houses on a hillside leading down to the sea but in fact is home to two-thirds of the island's population, at around midday and make our way down to the ship's car deck to wait for the large rear door to be lowered open. It's still probably the best part of a metre from touching down on the jetty's surface when a seaman grabs our bags and throws them to a colleague on the shore. Clearly used to this procedure, he catches them expertly and places them on the ground. Then, still with a foot or so to go, the seaman almost pushes us off the ship. We jump, and land on the concrete with a splash in the ship's wake, then turn to see the door being raised again and the *Aqua Spirit* heading back out to sea. It hasn't actually stopped and has made this port of call just for us.

Nikos, our landlord for the next three nights at the Maistrali Taverna and Studios, is waiting for us on the quayside with his ancient battered silver Toyota. He's a shortish, handsome man of about forty with black hair that's greying at the temples and, Barbara tells me dreamily, beautiful deep blue eyes. He loads the Toyota and drives us the few hundred metres up the hill to Maistrali, invites us to sit down on the balcony of his taverna and brings us a cold beer. We suspect that our room's not ready, but we're more than happy to sit and enjoy the view over the little port and across the bay towards Naxos.

And then, when we're midway through our drinks, Barbara lets out a small shriek. "Oh no," she says, "I've left my jacket on the ship." It was a chilly morning when we left Paros.

Nikos, who has been standing nearby talking to another man, is instantly aware that Barbara has a problem and offers to help. We explain our dilemma and he immediately pulls out his mobile phone and makes a call.

"What colour was it?" he asks after a while.

"Bright yellow," Barbara answers.

"And where did you leave it?"

We explain that we'd been sitting in the lounge, near the bar, for the whole of the journey and Nikos presumably relays the information to whoever he is talking to. And then he tells us, "Someone will ring me back."

We stay on the balcony and order lunch. And when he brings our bill for fourteen euros fifty Nikos informs us that the missing jacket has been located and that it will be delivered to the island on tomorrow morning's *Express Skopelitis* ferry. We're not altogether convinced, but in Greece you just never know.

Up in our smart spacious room which has a similar view over the port and across the bay, we're confronted with one of the perennial problems of Greek holiday accommodation – too few power points. In the main living area there are three that we can locate, one behind the bed, one behind a bedside table and the third under the dining table. Without moving furniture, we have no way of recharging anything or of plugging in the iPod and speakers.

Nikos's taverna, where we have dinner, has the atmosphere of an English village pub – when English villages used to have pubs with atmosphere, that is. Local men come and go, walking in, helping themselves to a beer or a Coke from the chiller, enjoying a plate of food, passing some time with other islanders, before leaving. And occasionally, very occasionally, money changes hands. Nikos seems to know them all well, which isn't difficult when there are only another hundred and fifty people living on the island. It could be that it's popular because there aren't many other places to go. Or because the food is excellent. Or simply because it's cheap. After a lunch that cost fourteen euros fifty, our dinner, including a litre of house red wine, comes to twenty-two euros.

*

For the first time since we left the UK two weeks ago, it's overcast and there's a little light rain. But at least the wind seems to have dropped. In a corner downstairs by the bar we find a decent strength wi-fi signal and book some accommodation on the island of Amorgos – and then Nikos appears with a plastic carrier bag containing Barbara's mislaid jacket. It had indeed been delivered on the little ferry that serves the Lesser Cyclades that we'd watched come and go from our balcony about an hour earlier.

The rain doesn't last long, and although it's not too hot everywhere dries out very quickly. Down in the village there's a little grocery shop that also serves as the post office and travel agency. It's dark and gloomy and looks as if it hasn't had a customer in years. The Royston Vasey shop of *The League of Gentlemen* comes to mind. The elderly man seated behind the counter, cigarette burning in an ashtray, is equally dark and gloomy and probably hasn't spoken to anyone in years either.

He certainly doesn't seem keen to speak to us. Happily, Barbara's Greek is good enough to make him understand what we want – tickets for Thursday afternoon's *Express Skopelitis* service to Amorgos – and he issues the tickets and takes our money without uttering a single word. The charm school classes were clearly a waste of money.

There are no buses or taxis on Iraklia, although Nikos has offered to chauffeur us around. But instead we embark on a two-hour walk that takes us around the west side of the island for two kilometres until we reach the deserted little beach resort of Livadia – which means 'beach' – before cutting inland and heading back to Agios Georgios to undo all the good the walk has done by lunching at the friendly, family-run Perigali taverna. And then we're treated to an incident that could have been taken from an episode of *Last of the Summer Wine*. We're walking back up the hill towards Maistrali when we spot two ageing pick-up trucks, with two equally ageing men standing between them, talking loudly. (Why do Greeks always sound as if they're arguing?) It's clear that one of the trucks has broken down and that the owner of the other one has offered to help out.

They have what looks like a line of knotted sheets but is presumably intended to serve as a towrope which they have attached to the back of the good truck. Then one of the men gets down on his stomach and attaches the other end to the front underside of the broken-down vehicle. After much tugging of the rope, they're satisfied that it is secure and they climb into their respective cabs and the driver of the towing truck starts his engine. He shouts something to the other driver, then inches slowly forward, the towrope tautens – and then the inevitable happens. Without the ailing truck moving as much as a centimetre, the rope snaps and the towing driver carries on for the best part of twenty metres before he realises he's not towing anything. We duck behind a wall and collapse in fits of laughter.

A few minutes later my mobile phone buzzes and my screen tells me my thirteen-year-old granddaughter Erin is the caller. She's recently developed this habit of going to school without her front door key and since we only live a couple of miles away I'm normally the one who's called to help.

"I'm sorry, darling, we're in Greece," I tell her. "Didn't your mum tell you?"

There's a brief silence at the other end, then, "Of course she did. Silly me. Sorry Granddad, have a nice holiday."

I text her half an hour later. She's waiting at a friend's house until her mother can get home.

*

There's only one other village on Iraklia, Panagia, nominally the island's capital. Panagia means 'all saints', and the village is named after its church. According to our guidebook it's about an hour's walk cross-country from Agios Georgios, so once the overnight wind and light rain have given way to a beautiful calm, sunny morning we decide to walk there. The route starts with a road leading upwards out of the village, which first turns into a wide dirt track and then into a well-worn footpath, for much of the way hedged on both sides by dense tall, dry grass. It's not difficult walking, and even at our leisurely pace we expect to make Panagia in about the suggested hour.

We've been walking for about half an hour and can see signs of a settlement in the distance when there's a rustling in the grass about two metres ahead of us on the left. And then it appears, slithering across the path and disappearing into the grass on the other side. We stand frozen, unable or unwilling to move. We've seen a snake in the wild once before. We were in a plantation garden outside Charleston, South Carolina, when this little thing wriggled across the path in front of us.

It wrapped itself around a sapling, bared its teeth and hissed at us. But it wasn't much bigger than a large earthworm and we stopped to photograph it, figuring that its bark, or hiss, was considerably worse than its bite. This, on the other hand, is an altogether different beast – sandy brown, probably four or five centimetres in diameter and at least a metre long. We look at each other and, without speaking, turn on our heels and head back towards Agios Georgios at a brisk pace.

An hour later, we're sitting outside a recently opened café bar with a beer to calm our nerves when another of those very Greek incidents occurs. An elderly man appears from a side street, shotgun tucked under his arm, and walks about fifty metres up the road before turning off to the right and vanishing from our sight. A couple of minutes later two loud shots ring out. No one else takes the slightest notice and we never do find out who or what has been shot.

The bar/restaurant area at Maistrali is busy again this evening, the food and drink as good as usual. We relate our snake experience to Nikos – whose response is an almost pitying smile.

"It was harmless," he says with a rare smile. "There are hundreds of them on the island."

We're intrigued by Nikos, a serious, seemingly intelligent man who appears to be at peace with himself and with the world and happy to be running a taverna and studios on a tiny island whose population is probably smaller than his IQ.

"Were you born on the island?" we ask when he brings our food.

Nikos shakes his head. "My father was born here," he says. "He moved to Athens and I was born there. We came back to Iraklia to run this place, oh, over twenty years ago now."

"Your English is very good. Did you learn in Athens?"

Another shake of the head. "I learn it here, from my guests."

As usual, locals come and go during the evening, having a drink, occasionally eating, seldom staying more than an hour. It's around nine-thirty when a young man enters carrying what looks like a plastic washing-up bowl covered with a tea towel. He puts it down on one of the tables and removes the towel, and two elderly men who have been sitting there for most of the evening nursing a glass of white wine pick up cutlery and begin attacking the bowl's contents with great enthusiasm, almost as if they haven't eaten for a week.

"What is it?" we ask one of the other customers, a young man who's noticed that we've been watching.

He quickly confers with his neighbour, then replies, "Sheep's head."

Today we spent the grand total of forty euros – twenty on lunch and twenty on dinner. There's not much else to spend money on here really.

CHAPTER SIX

Amorgos – "A pile of stones"

Today's Small Cyclades Lines ferry service doesn't call at Agios Georgios until three-thirty this afternoon and Nikos has said we can stay in the studio as long as we want. We're tempted to cancel our tickets and stay here for ever. Iraklia is the sort of idyllic island that persuades romantic Western Europeans with hippy inclinations to give up everything at home to come and live here. And if you can get by without daily newspapers, decent English-language TV, cask ale, public transport and reliable wi-fi, why not?

After another delicious lunch of "lamb in the oven", Nikos gets out the ancient Toyota once again and drives us back down to the port, wishes us farewell and goes back to Maistrali to collect two more guests who are also leaving the island. For the first time on this tour, our ferry leaves on time. It's a beautiful afternoon now, and we sit in the warm sunshine on the upper deck of the *Express Skopelitis* and enjoy what is effectively a two-hour cruise to Amorgos, the easternmost of the Cyclades, making brief stops at the little islands of Schinoussa and Koufonissi on the way.

The *Express Skopelitis* docks virtually in the centre of Katapola, the main port town of Amorgos, among the luxury cruisers and smaller flotilla yachts that are moored in the harbour. We're greeted on the quayside by a smiling elderly woman who speaks very little English but manages to make us understand that she's something to do with Pension Sofia, our next base. (We discover later that she's Evaggelia, mother of the eponymous Sofia and matriarch of the Nomikou family that seems to own half of the businesses in the village.) She leads us away from the waterside and up a cobbled, stepped path for about five minutes, then hands us over to a younger woman who speaks excellent English and introduces herself as Sofia.

Another couple of hundred metres wheeling our bags over the cobbles and we reach the Pension Sofia. We're on the ground floor of a square two-storey block, in a quiet, sheltered corner next to a small garden. There's a little enclosure, about a metre square with a low concrete wall around it in which dwell two tortoises, an ornamental pump that doesn't work and an opened half-empty tin of dark blue paint with which someone has recently been decorating some of the inanimate objects in the garden. Behind the fence and the fig trees we can hear chickens clucking, as well as the odd cow and goat, less mournful than their Folegandros cousin. The room's a decent size, although a little dark due to its secluded position, and, despite the assurances we've been given, without wi-fi.

It's busy when we go back to the taverna-lined waterfront later, probably as busy as anywhere in the islands we've been so far. We go to the fish restaurant Akrogiali and enjoy some wonderful seafood. (There seems to be an Akrogiali everywhere we've been in Greece, apart from Athens presumably, since it means 'sea side'.) We've taken an instant liking to Amorgos, and particularly Katapola, and we like it even more when we wander up one of the little side streets and find a shop selling today's

European editions of English daily newspapers. What bliss! A *Times* crossword to accompany my late-night Metaxa.

*

If we're going to move off Amorgos at some point in the near future we're going to need the internet to find accommodation, which means going up a flight of external stairs to the balcony outside Reception to get a wi-fi signal. Up here also happens to be where Evaggelia lives, and we've been here for no more than a couple of minutes – and learned from the net that the actor Roger Moore has died at the age of eighty-nine – when she appears. She wishes us a cheerful "Kalimera" and disappears inside. A minute or two later she reappears with two glasses of chilled fresh orange juice and tells us something in a mixture of Greek and English. The only words we can really understand are "techniko" and "later" but it's enough to have us believe we might get some wi-fi in our room before too long.

The same American travel magazine that waxed so lyrical about Folegrandros more recently described Amorgos as "possibly the fairest Greek island of them all." Katapola is a pretty port town with a population of about four hundred and fifty – or three times the population of the entire island of Iraklia – spread around a horseshoe-shaped bay. The island's capital, Chora (what else?), is similarly sized and several kilometres away in the hills. It's a rugged, dramatic landscape rising seven hundred metres up from the sea, and it's only about twenty years since it's been possible to cross the island from north to south by road, most people previously getting about by the little rowing boats known as caiques. Sadly, this summer's regular bus services don't start until the day we're planning to move on, so to do the one thing everyone who comes to Amorgos *must* do – visit the Monastery of Chozoviotissa – we'll need either a friendly taxi driver or a hire car. And since we can't find one of the former, friendly or otherwise, we go into Hermes Vehicle Rental (prop. Sofia Nomikou – she, or the family, also own a minimarket and a souvenir shop), shell out the princely sum of twenty euros and hire a Fiat Panda for tomorrow. And then we settle down outside a taverna and enjoy a cold beer.

For the past few years I've been one of an informal group of male friends who meet every month or so in a Brighton restaurant. We've all known each other since our children were at primary school together – in fact one of our number was the school's head teacher – and these days we sit down over breakfast and a coffee or two and put the world to rights. As we now enjoy the noon sun, a gathering at an adjoining taverna reminds me how our Greek contemporaries do it every day of the week. They sit outside the local kafenion nursing a coffee, an ouzo and a glass of water and argue loudly. At least it always sounds as though they're arguing. From time to time we hear a word we recognise, like Tsipras or Panathinaikos, but other than that we have no idea why they're so passionate. "If we lived in Greece," Barbara says quietly, "you lot could get together every day."

We have lunch at Viktoras Grill House on the waterside, where an A-board proudly advertises 'Cooked stuff', and enjoy a free local liqueur at the end of the meal, and when we return to the Pension Sofia there's a dish of six freshly laid eggs waiting for us on the chair outside our door, compliments of the management. The kindness of strangers again. But still no wi-fi.

*

It's windy and overcast first thing this morning, but by the time we collect our car and set off for Chozoviotissa the sky has largely cleared and it's another beautiful day. It's a journey of about ten kilometres along typical white-knuckle Greek island roads, a series of hairpin bends linked by thirty-metre straights, with no fences or barriers and precipitous drops where the tarmac ends. We go up and across the island, bypass Chora, then turn off and head down a narrower, equally twisting road until the monastery comes into view – a view which no amount of guidebook reading prepares you for and which is one of the most astonishing and breath-taking sights in the Cyclades.

The whitewashed monastery is embedded into the orange rock, halfway up the five-hundred-metre almost vertical cliff face. It was founded around 800AD by monks from Chozova, near Jericho, who had fled the Middle East with an icon said to have been decorated by St Luke. Rebuilt two hundred years later, the monastery was home to as many as a hundred monks in its heyday in the seventeenth century, although there are now only three of them, guarding religious icons and other works of art that, if they were sold and the proceeds donated to the state, could probably pay off Greece's debts to the EU. Down in the car park I make sure we're not being watched, then change out of my shorts and into a more respectful pair of chinos and we begin the three hundred and twenty-six step climb to the monastery door.

Twenty minutes later, tired and sweaty, we enter the monastery via a door that's barely as big as the one on our understairs cupboard at home and are greeted, rather solemnly, by one of the three monks, a tall, late-middle-aged man with the long grey hair and long grey beard of a Greek priest. The rooms we are allowed to see are small and dimly lit, their walls covered with all manner of paintings and icons. One of the 'civilians' on duty welcomes us more warmly and proudly describes the monastery's history and that of some of its contents, most of which date back to the seventeenth century. He points out one particular item which we assume is the icon said to have been decorated by St Luke, although we discover later that art historians believe it comes from the early ninth century. Protected by a glass screen, it's a highly polished plate, made from what looks like brass but is probably gold, about the size of an A4 sheet of paper, on which can be made out an etching of Christ. The monastery, he tells us, has not many months ago turned down an offer to buy it from the Louvre. The Paris museum was willing to pay eighteen million euros, but for reasons best known to themselves the monks politely declined.

We feel incredibly privileged to be here – until the man tells us that in the high season six or seven hundred people make the strenuous climb up the cliff every day. But they probably don't get the personal treatment we're having. He sits us down in an office and plies us with cool water, raki and delicious loukoumi, the Greek version of Turkish delight, before thanking us profusely for visiting and wishing us well. We stuff a couple of notes in a collection box and squeeze our way out through the doll's house door.

We stop and explore the narrow little streets and alleyways of Chora, have a drink in the pretty plane-tree-shaded square, then let the car freewheel its way back down into Katapola, where we have lunch on the waterside and watch the comings and goings of the smart young sailors from the two Hellenic Navy warships that have docked since we left the port earlier. The breeze has completely cleared the cloud that has shrouded the top of the island for much of the past two days and the dramatic hillsides dotted with tiny white churches are visible in all their glory. The Navy leaves, once the sailors have finished their lunchtime gyros and Cokes it appears, and it's just us and the, mainly French, yachties again. It truly is a good time to be in Greece.

*

I once had a friend, by his own admission not the world's most
ardent fan of ancient history and culture, who during a family
holiday in Turkey was persuaded by his then wife to hire a car
for a day so that they could visit the ancient ruins at Ephesus.
"How was it?" I asked him on their return home. "Half a day
sweating my b******s off in a tiny car just to see a pile of f******
stones," was his verdict. "Not too impressed then?" I replied.
Our experience this morning reminds me of that conversation.

Since we've been in Katapola we've been seeing signs that
read "Minoa 2k." The 'techniko' had clearly visited the Pension
Sofia while we were out yesterday because when we're woken by
the church bells at seven this morning we discover that we have
wi-fi in our room. We check online and learn that above the
town are what are described as the "impressive ruins of ancient
Minoa." According to Wikipedia, it was settled in the tenth
century BC, fortified as an acropolis and not abandoned until the
fourth century AD. Walls, parts of the acropolis, a gymnasium
and the remains of a temple to Apollo can still be seen. (Amorgos
has apparently yielded up many treasures, including the largest
Cycladic figurine in the National Archaeological Museum in
Athens.) After breakfast we set off to visit it.

It's hard work at times. The path is in places steep, uneven
and overgrown and it's hot under the late morning sun. It takes
us more than an hour to cover the alleged two kilometres but
we are rewarded with spectacular views over the island and the
Aegean Sea, and apart from the incessant buzz of insects it's
as silent as the grave. When we reach what we assume are the
"impressive ruins" they're unmarked. There's a broken-down
wire fence around the site and there had been an information
board there once but the information has been washed, worn
or blown away. Slightly more impressive than my friend's
"pile of stones," but overgrown, disorganised and pretty much
inaccessible. Which bits are the gymnasium and which the

temple to Apollo it's impossible to say. Two French tourists, who have taken the easy option and driven around the mountain to within about a hundred metres of the site, scratch their heads, wonder if they've come to the right place and wander back down to their car. We spend some time taking in the wonderful views, get some photos as evidence that we've been here, then head back down to Katapola for a beer.

CHAPTER SEVEN

Naxos – The priest's day off

The *Aqua Spirit*, the Nel Lines ferry that took us from Paros to Iraklia and on which Barbara left her yellow jacket, normally leaves Katapola for Naxos at one-thirty on Monday afternoons. We would have taken it, but, for a reason that the guy in the travel agency didn't explain to us, today's sailing has been cancelled, leaving us with the choice of *Express Skopelitis* or Blue Star's *Naxos*, both of which leave at 6am. We've plumped for the larger *Naxos* and what appears to be a shorter and cheaper journey – as well as its being a genuine car ferry with comfortable lounges and somewhere we can get breakfast. We've woken with the alarm at four-thirty, rattled our way over the cobbles down to the port area and boarded the ferry, all in the pre-dawn darkness. And then we've watched the sun rise over a flat calm sea on what has become a beautiful morning as we sail away from Amorgos.

Less than an hour later the *Naxos* is being manoeuvred into the tiny harbour at Koufonissi and an hour after that it's reversing into Agios Giorgios, on Iraklia. We've gone up to the top deck to watch the comings and goings – it's somewhat busier than when we came here a week ago; the ship's docked properly and people are actually getting on and off – and down on the quayside we spot our erstwhile landlord Nikos. We wave frantically until he recognises Barbara's yellow jacket and waves back. We have a friend for life, we feel.

On the quayside at Naxos, where we arrive at a little after nine o'clock, Stathis, our landlord at the Athina Studios, is waiting for us. A tall, slim fifty-something on a crutch to support a right knee which is encased in an uncomfortable-looking metal brace, he is holding what looks like a shoe-box lid with "Barbra" (*sic*) scrawled untidily in felt-tip across it. The journey through the narrow, crowded streets of Naxos town's one-way system to Athina, at the opposite end of the seafront to the port area, in yet another battered silver Toyota, takes about fifteen minutes, during most of which time Stathis is engaged in an animated conversation on his mobile phone.

Because it's so early our room isn't ready. We leave our luggage in the reception area and Stathis invites us onto his private balcony where he plies us with strong Greek coffee and opens out a map to point out places we should be seeing while we're on Naxos. On our two previous brief visits we'd assumed there wasn't much to the island other than the seafront area in Naxos town and the ruined castle up above – apart from the unfinished Temple of Apollo, a 2,500-year-old doorway to nowhere on a little islet connected to the mainland by a narrow causeway. It greets you as you arrive in the port like a giant croquet hoop, the best-known and most important archaeological site on the island. But this is the largest of the Cyclades, Byron's favourite allegedly, and as Stathis confirms, there's bound to be more to see.

We have a pre-lunch drink at a café on the seafront, where Barbara's glass of white wine is as big as my beer, then seek out Moro, a taverna in the back streets that has been recommended by Stathis. The owner welcomes us warmly and serves us more food than we can eat, and when he brings us the bill for fourteen-fifty he gives us an extra half-litre of barrel rosé "on the house".

*

Across the road from our studio at Athina there's a small modern hotel in which a group of about fifteen British men and women are staying. They're all people of around our own age, that's to say in their sixties, and appear to be on an organised walking holiday. They have their communal breakfast on the hotel's terrace at precisely eight each morning, noisy and excited about the day ahead, then, sturdy-booted and armed with small rucksacks and walking poles, they leave in a small coach at nine. As we breakfast on our own balcony, a middle-aged woman on an ancient bicycle wobbles dangerously as she crosses herself while cycling past the little church opposite. Across the strait that separates Naxos and Paros, Blue Star Lines' *Delos* is heading towards us. Olympic Airlines planes occasionally come into the island airport that's just a few kilometres away to our left. There's a slight breeze that keeps the temperature bearable but it's a beautiful morning.

The little village of Chalki, our first stop on a bus journey through the island, was the capital of Naxos until 1925, and when you look at a map it's easy to understand why. It's situated at the very geographical heart of the island. It's also the home of one of Naxos's most important churches, the Protothronos, built in the twelfth century and allegedly full of ancient Byzantine frescoes. But for reasons known only to the authorities, and despite what it says in our guidebook, the church remains locked when it's not being used for services. If you can find a priest you can, apparently, persuade him to open up and let you see the paintings. We're told that the priest's frequently seen around the village. Today, however, he appears to be having a day off.

49

Chalki itself has become twee and a little hippyfied, but it is in the centre of a fertile valley where olives and the large lemon-like citrons are cultivated. The local liqueur Kitron Naxos has been made to a secret family recipe in the village since 1896 and we take the opportunity to visit the Vallindra distillery, the first and only place it's ever been made legally. From the thimble-sized sample we're given, we can tell it's very sweet – too sweet to tempt us into buying any – and, we're informed, quite potent. It was a fashionable drink for Athenians in the 1980s, we're told by our guide, but virtually unknown today outside Naxos.

The bus up to the next village, Filoti, the largest settlement in the region, is half an hour late, but once there we're able to settle down outside a bar, enjoy a cold beer and watch the villagers go about their business. And then we pick up the bus again and take the switchback ride to what Stathis has assured us is the jewel in the island's crown, Apiranthos. High in the hills, it was originally built by Cretan settlers in the tenth century who came to Naxos to work in Greece's only emery mines. Naxos's reputation as a producer of emery is such that in Roman times the mineral was known as 'naxium', and it was only in the mid-nineteenth century that substantial deposits were discovered in Turkey and the island's dominance in the industry was challenged. Today, a handful of people still work the mines for a couple of months every year, and what's left of the workings has been placed under a preservation order by the Ministry of Culture. Wonderful to think that the fashion for smart fingernails has played its part in the heritage of the Cyclades.

Apiranthos has the reputation of being the most picturesque village on Naxos, all narrow winding paths paved with marble, car-free, with interesting shops and spectacular views over the eastern side of the island. Byron was here as well, and he loved the village so much he said he wanted to die here (he didn't – he died at Missolonghi on the mainland in 1824). Women weave at looms outside their houses, farmers sell their produce by the bus stop at the edge of the village. It's a wonderful place to sit and chill over a late lunch, proof that there is so much more to this island than the lively, noisy and at times tacky Chora that greets you when you get off the ferry.

Chapter Eight

Mykonos – "Convenient for the night scene"

The *Naxos Star* doubles as a ferry and an excursion boat, and when we were in the Cyclades in 2007 we had several trips on it. The first was from Mykonos, where our flight from Gatwick landed, to Paros. The second was an excursion from Paros to Santorini, the third back to Mykonos to get our flight home. Since then it has attracted huge numbers of comments on TripAdvisor, most of them about how uncomfortable people's journeys were and how many, if not most, of their fellow passengers had been sick. We did experience two or three bumpy journeys back then, but it's not a very big boat and the Cyclades region is known for its strong winds and rough seas, so we'd half-expected it. Today, however, it's a beautiful morning and the sea is as calm as the proverbial millpond. We're travelling to Mykonos, via Delos, and we're not expecting any discomfort – at least not from the elements.

The ever-helpful Stathis has driven us to the port area, and our nine o'clock sailing gets under way at nine-fifteen. *Naxos Star* holds about two hundred people and is probably about half-full when it leaves Naxos. We head across the strait and pull into the little harbour at Naoussa, on Paros, where a remarkable scene is being played out. On the quayside are probably a hundred people, many of them French and most of them middle-aged and older. A solitary policeman has erected a flimsy tape barrier to try and stop them from spilling over the edge of the quay and into the water. They push and jostle impatiently like refugees waiting for a boat to take them to safety as the ship reverses up to the concrete jetty, then they burst through the tape and almost run up the gangway as soon as it's lowered. We've stowed our luggage at the front of the ship and chosen a quiet, comfortable spot on the top, outdoor deck, but within seconds of the ship docking at Naoussa we're hemmed in on all sides by noisy, restless French tourists, many of whom, because we're outside, decide it's OK to smoke.

Happily, it's less than two uncomfortable hours to the tiny sacred island of Delos, once the hub of the Cyclades and now a large open-air museum, completely deserted apart from the Ministry of Culture employees who guard the ruins and the boatloads of day-trippers. Eroded and treeless, it's said to have been the birthplace of the divine twins Apollo and Artemis, the unique remains of an entire city that was once home to thirty thousand people undisturbed by modern building. Apart from the museum, that is, housing one of the best collections of Greek sculptures and offering interesting insights into ancient domestic life.

It's a Unesco World Heritage Site, with ruins dating back to 1400 BC, but in true Greek fashion it's a little overgrown in places and in urgent need of some serious TLC. The Ancient Greeks allowed no burials on the island, but that doesn't prevent it from being haunted by the memories of a once-great empire. Today no one is allowed to stay here overnight, and apart from the overpriced café near the museum, it pays scant attention to hospitality. But it's mind-bogglingly wonderful, even though the French tourists who made our journey from Paros so uncomfortable seem hell-bent on rushing round the island as quickly as possible and snatching a few selfies so they can get back to the *Naxos Star* to grab the best seats. It's a never-to-be-forgotten experience, and the bruises we've picked up from the tourists who tried to push past us in the queue to get in will soon fade. And the lizards are amazing, scuttling all over the island and the biggest we've ever seen in Greece.

*

The *Naxos Star* reaches the old harbour in Mykonos town in mid-afternoon. We wheel our bags around the water's edge and find the Manto Hotel, our home for the next two days, in a little side street just off the main square. (In the square there is a bust of the eponymous Manto, a heroine of the Greek War of Independence with the surname Mavrogenous.) According to our guidebook, the hotel is "convenient for connoisseurs of the night scene," but that's not really why Barbara chose it. "Convenient" is enough for us. We originally weren't sure about staying on Mykonos at all, given its current reputation, but we've reasoned that in order to get the whole picture of the Cyclades we have to see places like this, as well as those like Iraklia.

Simple, unadorned Greece it most definitely is not. The increase in tourism may have caught some other Greek islands unawares, but not Mykonos, which since *Shirley Valentine* was filmed here in the late 1980s has gone from being one of the poorest, most barren of Greek islands to become the most popular island in the Cyclades, dedicated to satisfying the whims of the mostly young and beautiful tourists from around the world who flock here in their thousands. It has become famous for its nightlife, its gay scene and its international cuisine – and its high prices. But as you approach the main town, Mykonos Chora, from the sea and see the row of seven restored thatched windmills on the Kato Myli hill overlooking the town you can't fail to be impressed by its beauty.

The tavernas on the northern quayside, the town's main promenade, are mostly expensive and occasionally pretentious. Uniquely for Greek islands, the staff who tout for business at many of them wear smart uniforms and their menus are imitation-leather-bound and printed rather than being the handwritten, you-can-have-whatever-we-happen-to-have-in-today variety. Waiters ostentatiously top up diners' wine glasses while keeping their non-pouring hand behind their back, sommelier-style. But we find somewhere more authentically Greek where we can get a late lunch and a drink for no more than twenty euros and settle down to do what many people who come here do, people-watch.

Mykonos in the evening is where people come out to wander around, to see and be seen. The narrow labyrinthine whitewashed streets, so designed to break the ever-present wind, are lined with dimly lit bars and brightly lit boutiques bearing names like Louis Vuitton, Dolce and Gabbana and Hermes. Young and not so young, simultaneously overdressed and underdressed women risk serious damage to their ankles as they totter over the uneven cobbles in their six-inch heels. It's supposed to be the hang-out of celebrities but we don't spot any. Or at least none that we recognise, and I suppose being recognised is the whole point of celebrity. Any or all of these women could be stars of *The Only Way Is Essex*, *Love Island*, *Made in Chelsea* or some other scripted reality TV show, but since we never watch anything like that we'll never know.

In a little square not far from the hotel we find Kostas taverna, one of the few really authentic-looking establishments in the centre of the town. We eat and drink for a reasonable twenty-five euros, but largely by eating and drinking not very much.

So far, despite the warnings, we've had no problems with ATMs dispensing cash, but we *are* on a budget. But then judging by some of the bodies parading past, not eating very much seems to be the norm here.

*

Given the Manto Hotel's alleged "convenience" for the "night scene," we've had a surprisingly good night's sleep. This is supposed to be a party island and we'd expected noise into the small hours, but it's been strangely quiet. Maybe it's not quite as convenient as the owners and the guidebook would have us believe. We've decided that there has to be more to Mykonos than its reputation would have you understand, so after a decent breakfast in the hotel's reception area we set out to see if we can find it.

On what is an overcast, sultry morning, we walk out of the heart of the town towards the new port, past a string of expensive-looking hotels and apartment complexes, until we arrive at what appears to be a new marina development. It's clearly been built to draw in the sailing fraternity that finds this part of the Mediterranean so attractive, but at the moment it seems to be singularly failing in that mission. In spite of the modern facilities, virtually nothing is moored there, least of all any of the floating gin palaces the developers were almost certainly expecting.

Nearby, in a sad contrast, there's a flimsy shelter made out of cardboard packaging and propped against the wall at the edge of the beach. A forlorn young North African woman dressed all in black sits next to it, staring out at the sea, while two small children sleep on the sand beside her. Next to them are two large filthy holdalls containing their world. There's no sign of the father of this little family but he's no doubt somewhere nearby hawking cheap plastic toys and bootleg DVDs to gullible tourists in an attempt to feed them. It's a sight that in any context would bring a tear to the eye of the hardest-hearted. Here, a few hundred metres from where the young and privileged are sleeping off the excesses of an evening's partying, it's poignant beyond measure.

Back in the town, we walk around the area known as Little Venice, where tall shabby houses on stilts appear to be about to fall into the sea. Anywhere less like Venice is hard to imagine. Once the homes of sailors and ship-owners, most now house trendy cocktail bars selling 33cl bottles of lager at six-fifty or seven euros, the most expensive we've ever seen in Greece. Even the fake designer sunglasses, fridge magnets and "a gift from Mykonos" coasters in the souvenir shops cost twice as much as on any other island.

In the old town, where life appears to be very much more genuinely Greek, we find a chaotic bar where we can get a 50cl draught beer for a more realistic two euros fifty and then some reasonably-priced and very good pita gyros. And as we make our way through the twisting little streets again, we turn a corner and almost bump into the only celebrity we do recognise – the singer Marc Almond, who appears to be lost and having a heated discussion with his male companion about which direction they should be taking. We resist the temptation to point them towards the airport and do something we suspect very few visitors to this island ever do – head for the Mykonos Archaeological Museum.

Opened in 1905 and said to be one of the oldest museums in Greece, the prison-like building houses a particularly impressive collection of ceramics. Richly decorated with sphinxes, lions, birds and horses, many of them have been brought over from Delos, although the most spectacular of all the exhibits was found on Tinos, the next island on our itinerary. It's a tall, seventh-century-BC funeral urn with relief scenes from the Fall of Troy, almost like a comic strip that shows the warrior-stuffed Trojan Horse compete with airplane-like windows. Why doesn't everyone come and spend some time here, we wonder?

This evening we eat at the Paraportiani taverna, next to the church after which it is named and which is one of Mykonos's architectural gems. There are, allegedly, four hundred churches in the town, some of them no bigger than broom cupboards, but the Panagia Paraportiani is the most famous, snow-white with four separate churches asymmetrically linked. It's a beautiful evening and a beautiful setting to have dinner and again we're able to eat for less than thirty euros – but again by not eating very much. We have a nightcap at Gialos, on the northern quayside, indulge in a little more people-watching and wonder whether we'll ever come back to Mykonos.

CHAPTER NINE

Tinos – The Lourdes of Greece

If it's possible to be depressed in Greece, we're close to it now as we prepare to leave Mykonos after our forty-eight-hour stay. Not sad for ourselves, but for those who visit the island, and particularly its main town, and who believe that Mykonos is Greece and that Greece is Mykonos. Apart from its stunning Cycladean beauty, it's about as far from the real Greece as it's possible to get, but hopefully we'll be back in that world soon. This morning, we pay two euros each to take the Mykonos Sea Bus, the local water taxi, from the northern quayside where the day trips to Delos start and finish to the new port, and board the large and very busy Blue Star Lines' *Paros*.

As we enter the ferry port at Tinos less than an hour later, we're surprised by the sheer scale of the facilities. Why on earth, we wonder, does a small island with a resident population of fewer than nine thousand souls need a huge, EU-funded passenger terminal with parking spaces for more than a thousand cars? The answer is that every year on a single day in March and another in August Tinos becomes the Lourdes of

Greece, occupying much the same place in the hearts of modern Greeks as Delos did in the hearts of their ancestors. Thousands of pilgrims descend on the island every Feast of the Assumption, 15th August, and the ceremonies that take place are broadcast live on Greek national television. The destination of all these pilgrims sits on a hill above the town, the yellow-painted neo-classical Panagia Evangelistria church, with a neon cross, that houses a miraculous icon.

According to Greek tradition, a nun, Sister Pelagia, twice had a vision of the Virgin Mary directing her to a rock where she discovered an icon. It was 1822, and the second year of the Greek War of Independence, and the holy discovery gave the freedom fighters a boost in morale. Furthermore, the icon, which depicted the Virgin Mary kneeling at prayer, was found to have remarkable healing powers. A church, the Panagia Evangelistria, or Our Lady of the Good Tidings, was built on the spot where it was discovered and it quickly became the most important pilgrimage site in Greece. During the regime of the Greek Colonels in the late 1960s and early 1970s, the entire island of Tinos was in fact declared holy as part of the military government's 'moral cleansing'.

Stories are rife throughout Greece of miracles attributed to visits to the Tinos icon. Disabled people being able to walk, visually impaired children seeing clearly, childless couples suddenly finding themselves expecting a baby. Many Greeks save for months to be able to visit Tinos and stay on the island for a single night. Some leave their small towns and villages to spend a night sleeping on the porch of the Panagia Evangelistria, so strong is their faith in the icon. Nowadays, it seems, the entire town is dedicated to capitalising on the story of the icon, and however much you read in advance nothing quite prepares you for it. It's a bizarre, unforgettable, moving and, we find, disturbing experience.

The hill on which the Panagia Evangelistria church stands is approached by two roads that cover the eight hundred metres from the waterside, a hundred metres apart at the start but gradually tapering until they converge in a square paved with pebbles in front of the church. One is Leoforos Megalocharis, a wide residential street that has a metre-wide carpet laid at the kerb at the right-hand side of the road as you ascend. Today, two workmen are busy replacing worn sections of the carpet, making it as comfortable as possible for the thousands of pilgrims who will crawl up it in a couple of months' time.

The other is Evangelistria Street, a thoroughfare that wouldn't be out of place in Blackpool or Las Vegas and the route we take to reach the church. It's tightly packed with small shops that are crammed to bursting with the tackiest souvenirs imaginable. Fridge magnets, bottle openers, ceramic nymph salt and pepper pots and seashell frogs playing pool mingle with Panagia thermometers, bottles of holy water, tin keyfob-sized votive items and candles that range from tea lights to slender six-feet-tall sticks at five euros each for lighting in the church. And many of these shops seem to be doing a lively trade with the Greek visitors.

Once we reach the top of the hill, we stand at the foot of the marble stairs, partly covered in red carpet, and admire the undoubtedly attractive church – and get our first evidence of the amazing drawing power of the icon. A woman, probably in her late thirties and wearing a tee-shirt, shorts and skateboarding kneepads, is crawling across the square. Accompanied by an older couple, who are probably her parents, and three young children, she makes her way slowly up the steps towards the church.

Out of respect to Greek traditions, and in compliance with the many signs around, I pull over my shorts the pair of chinos I've been carrying in my rucksack while Barbara covers her legs with a wrap-around skirt, and we follow the family up the steps to the church. But we wonder why we've bothered with the extra clothes, since shorts and bare shoulders seem not to raise a single eyebrow and are almost the order of the day. At the door of the church we join a line of visitors – a mixture of Greeks and excitable Asian tourists taking selfies – which we assume is the queue to get in. We move forward slowly, and it's only when we're inside that we realise we're actually in the queue to kiss the icon. We step aside and discreetly watch the proceedings.

The icon itself is encased in gold and silver and so smothered in precious stones that it's almost impossible to see the dark outline of the Virgin's face. But the line, mostly of Greek women, continues to shuffle up to it, lean up to kiss it and then cross themselves, before backing away, frenziedly crossing themselves again and looking for something else to kiss. Through the smoke and incense, the church is like an Aladdin's cave with hundreds of votive items hanging from the ceiling and from everything on which it's possible to hang something. Tin reproductions of hearts, ears, pairs of lungs, limbs, all bear witness to what has been healed by visiting the church – or what the person who left the votive believes *will be* healed. A truck, a ship, a bucket – previously blind pilgrims have given the icon a symbol of the first thing they saw when their sight was restored. It's difficult not to make comparisons with Christmas decorations, but we do our best not to.

Back outside in the bright sunlight we watch as an elderly woman dressed head to foot in black crawls up the last few steps then joins the queue at the church door, still on her hands and knees, to kiss the icon. Further down Leoforos Megalocharis another middle-aged woman is sobbing uncontrollably as she makes slow progress along the kerbside carpet. Her tears, we learn later, are almost certainly tears of joy, of gratitude that her prayers have been answered, however, and nothing at all to do with the fact that she is probably in some considerable discomfort from already having crawled the best part of half a mile uphill from the quayside.

At the bottom of the hill we park ourselves at a taverna, enjoy a light lunch of fried little fish and a Greek salad and a half-litre of house white, and quietly reflect on the remarkable, raw scenes we've just witnessed. And then we haul our bags bag to the ferry terminal to await Blue Star Lines' ship *Patmos* that will take us to Syros.

CHAPTER TEN

Syros – "There's no culture left"

We've decided to stay on Syros, the eleventh (if you include Ios) and last island in our Cyclades odyssey, a little longer than we've stayed anywhere else so far. After over a month's travelling, we're starting to feel a little tired (or at least I am) and need a short break to recharge our batteries. Ermoupoli, the capital of Syros and, in fact, of the Cyclades, is described in our guidebook as the "best-preserved nineteenth-century neo-classical town in the whole of Greece." Because of its large natural harbour, it was Greece's busiest port until it was eclipsed by Piraeus in the late nineteenth century, and as we approach on the ferry from Tinos on a beautiful late Saturday afternoon it's an imposing and somewhat unexpected sight. The town rises in two peaks from the harbour. To our left is the older quarter, Ano Syros, Upper or Old Syros, topped with the Catholic cathedral of St George. To the right is Vrondado, founded during the War of Independence and crowned by the Byzantine church Anastasis. Ahead of us as we steam into the harbour are the rusting cranes of the Neorion shipyard and the idle rusting shells of several old ships that are no longer under repair.

We disembark and pull our bags along the waterfront towards the town centre with no real idea of where we're going. Eventually, we hail a passing taxi and show the driver the piece of paper on which Barbara has written the name and address of our accommodation, Konstanza Studios. He looks at it, nods and puts our luggage into the boot. When we're safely in the back seat he pulls off the seafront road into the densely developed maze of narrow back streets. After about two minutes he stops and makes a phone call. The only words we recognise are the name of the street and "ne" or "yes" repeated several times. Another two minutes later he turns into a street barely wide enough for his Mercedes, stops, jumps out of the car and removes our bags from his boot. He seems more than happy with the five-euro note we give him and drives off.

We're left standing at the foot of a wide staircase that leads to a first floor landing. A sign beside the open double door tells us that this is indeed Konstanza Studios, and before we can begin to scale the stairs a small, smiling sixty-something woman appears on the landing and beckons us up with a welcoming sweep of her right arm. It is Konstanza herself, and even though she speaks virtually no English we all make ourselves understood, and it isn't long before we're unpacking in a large first floor room with a balcony that seems to hang halfway across the narrow street.

We're down in the street a little later, and outside the corner shop where we buy a few provisions we bump into the smiling Konstanza again. We have a map of Ermoupoli that we picked up on the ferry, and, using one of her fingers, Konstanza traces out the shortest route on foot between here and the town centre. We follow the route as closely as we can remember it when we go out in the evening. It takes us through narrow back streets, up and down flights of steps, through squares and past two large churches until, after about fifteen minutes, it delivers us to the harbour.

The crescent-shaped waterfront area is probably the best part of a kilometre in length and is lined with the tables and chairs of the restaurants, all of whose kitchens are on the other side of a busy road. The harbour itself is full of boats, everything from small yachts rented by Western European sailing tourists to the massive craft owned by, we're told, Russian oligarchs. On the decks of the latter, groups of smartly dressed overweight middle-aged men and young glamorous women sit at tables and are served dinner and drinks by young crew members in brilliant white uniforms. Do they ever get off these floating gin palaces to visit the places they dock at, we wonder? Do they even know where they are?

We settle down at a simple taverna and enjoy one of the best meals we've had so far, at less than twenty-seven euros including our wine. The road that separates our table from the taverna's kitchen is alive with Greeks enjoying Saturday evening. Families promenade from one end of the harbour to the other. Young men in old cars cruise first in one direction, and then in the other. Groups of motorcyclists roar up and down. The occasional bus makes a point of letting car drivers know that they're parked too near the corners and making life difficult. Taverna staff risk their lives ferrying food and drink back and forth across the road. As I fall asleep later watching the *Eurovision Song Contest* on our television at Konstanza Studios, I reflect that life doesn't really get much better.

*

Apart from various sets of church bells ringing at irregular intervals, it's a calm, quiet Sunday morning. It seems that Portugal won the *Eurovision Song Contest* that I fell asleep while watching last night, a singer called Salvador Sobral with a song called 'Amar Pelos Dios'. The British entry, Lucie Jones, managed a creditable 111 points and finished fifteenth with 'Never Give Up On You'. Greece, which still takes the competition seriously, finished nineteenth, thanks largely to the votes of her neighbour Albania and her cousins in Cyprus.

Ermoupoli on a beautiful early summer Sunday morning is a wonderful place to be. In the central square, Plateia Miaoulis, families and couples are out for a stroll across the shining Cyclades marble pavement. Said to be the most elegant nineteenth-century square in Greece, it's named after the revolutionary hero and admiral Andreas Miaoulis, whose statue forms its centrepiece and looks imperiously down Venizelou Street to the harbour. On the northern side is the massive neo-classical Dimarcheion, or town hall, designed by the German architect Ernst Ziller and reached by a broad flight of marble stairs. All around are tall palm trees and fine buildings with wrought-iron balconies. Less famous but no less beautiful than St Mark's Square in Venice or St Peter's in Rome, it seems like a special place to be.

Down on the harbourfront we find another unexpected delight – a souvenir shop selling this morning's English newspapers. We buy a *Sunday Times* (something of an extravagance at five euros fifty), cross the ever-busy road and settle down for an hour with a strong coffee and an in-depth look at what's happening back at home. We're surrounded by Greeks doing the same, apart from reading the *Sunday Times*, of course. What sort of market there is here for English newspapers is difficult to fathom. Syros is most certainly not on the radar of any British tour operators we know, and what tourism there is seems to be predominantly domestic.

It's at times like these that you realise how important the inter-island ferries are to the local people. Hellenic Seaways'

67

Artemis docks not far away from where we're sitting and disgorges dozens of foot passengers and cars, followed by truck after truck laden with all manner of goods. Inhabitants of Syros call the island 'our rock', and it's as dry and barren as you can imagine. Almost all the food and drink consumed here has to be imported and the ships are, quite literally, a lifeline.

*

The virtual wall-to-wall sunshine that we've been enjoying these past four weeks may not last. According to BBC Weather, which we pick up on the iPad, there could be some severe storms on the way. A still-fine Monday morning is time to begin exploring this beautiful little island. We make our way down to the waterfront, where a sign on the harbour wall warns, in English, of "Danger – because of big undulations from going through boats and bad weather conditions," then head across the Plateia Miaoulis again until we come to the opulent Vaporia district. It's a stark contrast to some of the other decaying corners of the town, all palm-lined squares and elegant mansions built by shipowners, many of which have been converted into boutique hotels – the mansions, that is, not the shipowners.

It's there that we find the Orthodox Agios Nikolaos church, built with the shipowners' wealth, grand and loaded with murals, icons, gilt and chandeliers and, like the monastery on Amorgos, housing enough treasures to settle the national debt. Or is it heresy to have thoughts like that?

From here we walk to the Vrondado, the residential area built on one of the two hills that dominate Ermopouli. It's a long, strenuous climb up a series of steep, stepped streets, probably the most difficult walk we've had since we arrived in the Cyclades. There's very little shade and frequent stops to get one's breath back are necessary. And when we get to the square at the top, the Anastasi, the Byzantine Church of the Resurrection, is frustratingly closed. The church houses some valuable icons which we'll never see, but at least it does have a tap outside with a sign inviting us to refill our water bottles, and spectacular views across the town and as far as Tinos and Mykonos – and the walk back down into the town is considerably easier.

Ermopouli was once one of the most important ship-building centres in the Mediterranean, but today the Neorion shipyard stands idle. Opened in 1861, it played a major role in the Cycladean economy for a century and a half, but today its gates are chained shut and draped in banners bearing slogans we can't read but assume aren't messages of support for the Government. It closed in 2014 when the Greek navy could no longer afford to keep awarding it contracts to repair its warships, and apart from the handful of redundant workers who keep a permanent vigil on the pavement outside, no one seems to care. It's a symbol of Ermoupoli's past, a symptom of Greece's present. And as if the point needing reinforcing, we remember a shiny brass plaque on Blue Star's *Patmos*, which brought us here the other day, informing us that the vessel had been built in South Korea.

When we have dinner in Stefanon Street this evening, we find ourselves next to a table of eight boisterous, noisy people of varying ages whose language, or dialect, we can't fathom. Inevitably, since there are very few other people out this evening, we fall into conversation with them. They turn out to be from Luxembourg – all eight of them ("Is there anyone left at home?" we ask. They take it well.) – and what they speak among themselves is their own curious form of German. They're on a week's sailing around the islands and tomorrow they're off to Mykonos. They all speak remarkable English, and when we ask how they manage to speak it so well one of the younger members of the group explains he was once a student in Leeds. By one of those amazing coincidences I discover he had lived in the same street as I'd lived in when I was a journalist in the city in the 1970s. We've bought our groceries in the same supermarket and drunk in the same pub. As we leave we wish them well – and warn them that they'll find life a little more expensive on Mykonos.

Back at Konstanza, the BBC website is still forecasting storms and temperatures of twenty or twenty-one, rather than the twenty-six to twenty-eight we've been enjoying. And, according to the news channels, Yanis Varoufakis is still predicting that if Greece is forced to leave the eurozone, the entire system will collapse.

*

It's another beautiful morning, no sign yet of the storms the BBC has forecast, although as the morning wears on some cloud does start to build up. It's sultry and, according to the indicator outside one of the pharmacies, twenty-eight degrees. We walk down to the street at the side of the shipyard, where a makeshift bus stop is temporarily replacing the one on the road outside the port, which is under repair or reconstruction. It's impossible to say which since for the entire time we're on the island we don't see any work going on.

The bus around the south of the island takes us past the island's little airport to what is said to be its finest beach, Vari. It is undoubtedly pretty and it's said to have first been settled in the Neolithic era. Today it seems to consist of little more than a row of tavernas and bars along the pale grey sandy beach, and it's almost deserted. We settle down, have a cold beer, admire the view and work out our next move.

Since there isn't another bus for at least two hours, and we don't particularly want to spend that long in Vari, we decide to walk to the next village on the coast. Megas Gialos appears to be about four kilometres away, and since it's along the coast road we reason that it will be relatively flat. And apart from the climb up from Vari Bay to the road, that's how it proves to be. After about an hour of fairly gentle walking we reach the outskirts of Megas Gialos and sit ourselves down outside a roadside taverna. A few locals come and go, some staying to enjoy a meal or a drink, others seemingly just to have a chat with the owner. It's one of those places where you wonder how they make a living, but the food's great, the service is friendly and efficient and the view is wonderful. And we just have time to settle our bill, visit the loos and hop across the road to get the next bus.

The bus takes us through the seaside villages of Komito, Angathorpes, Posidonia and Finikas until we cut across a headland and stop in Galissas, on the west of the island. Our guidebook tells us that it "has seen better days," and it does seem to have something of a lived-in, slightly run-down air about it. But the comments don't appear to have put off the Greek families who are out in their numbers enjoying the wide sandy beach and good collection of cafés and tavernas. It's an excellent place to pass the time before picking up the bus again and crossing the island at its highest point back to Ermoupoli.

On the walk back to our accommodation we spot a particularly interesting butcher's shop. We buy about half a tonne of chicken breasts for two euros fifty and decide to eat in for a change, stopping at a nearby minimarket for some vegetables. It proves to be an inspired decision. As we walk the final few hundred metres back to our accommodation, the sky becomes grey and heavy, the wind increases in speed and we realise that the storm could at last be on its way. It's about seven o'clock when the rain starts, just a few spots at first but with a couple of claps of thunder in the distance. By around eight the sky is pitch-black, apart from when it's lit up by spectacular lightning flashes. It rains heavily for most of the evening and we enjoy our chicken casserole.

*

The storm has raged through most of the night, the lightning strikes sometimes scarily close, and the morning sky is grey and cloudy with only small patches of pale blue where the sun tries to break through. Further storms are forecast. We don't come to Greece simply for the weather but, like everywhere else, it all looks so much better when the sun is shining. Sadly, this morning it doesn't look so great. It continues to rain on and off and so we do what Brits abroad tend to do when the weather isn't brilliant – we go to a museum. Not just any museum, though, but the jewel in Ermoupoli's crown. In a restored factory just outside the town centre, the Industrial Museum of Ermoupoli houses a collection that chronicles Syros's past as one of the main commercial centres of the eastern Mediterranean.

It has dozens of well-labelled items telling the stories not just of shipbuilding, but of printing, spinning, engine building and a host of other trades. It also has next door the fascinating Aneroussis lead shot factory, to which we and another British couple are lucky to be given a guided tour. It was clearly a very dangerous place to work. Our guide, a passionate and knowledgeable middle-aged man who explains how the lead shot was made and the alarming daily hazards faced by the workers, is rightly proud of his island's history, if a little depressed and cynical about its present.

"There is no culture on this island anymore," he says in answer to one of our questions. "Everyone who has culture has gone to Athens." Anyone with any get-up-and-go, he says, has, well, got up and gone. "The young people who are left have an Anatolian attitude. They are lazy. They don't care about the past. They just think of themselves." By Anatolian he means Turkish.

After a light lunch in the town centre we try and make sense of how the round-the-town bus service works – and fail miserably. As do the Greek/German couple with whom we share a taxi to Ano Syros. The medieval Catholic quarter of Ermoupoli towers over the rest of the town and is reached by local bus, taxi or the eight hundred and seventy cobbled steps that someone once took the trouble to count. The hill, a pedestrian-only labyrinth of whitewashed alleys and archways, tapers to a point, topped with the pink-roofed Cathedral of St George, or Ai-Giogri. Herman Melville, the man who wrote *Moby Dick*, came here in the middle of the nineteenth century and wrote that the houses clung around the top of the hill "like shipwrecked men about a rock." We wonder if, like us, he found the cathedral closed.

It has for some years apparently been undergoing extensive refurbishment and renovation and is surrounded by a tall metal fence. A solitary young female stonemason chips away with her chisel, looks up, greets us with a smiling "Yasas" and carries on with her work. We tour the perimeter fence, then begin to make our way back down to sea level. Some of the little stepped streets have been turned into waterfalls by the sporadic heavy showers but we manage to keep our feet dry. We linger in a square at the bust of local hero Markos Vamvakaris, a pioneer of the bouzouki and of rebetiko music who was born up here in 1905 and after whom the square is named. "Your eyelashes shine like the flowers of the meadow" – so begins his best-known song. Since rebetiko is only slightly less of a dirge than the Portuguese *fado*, Vamvakaris's music probably doesn't get too many downloads on Spotify.

A little further down, the sixteenth-century Church of Our Lady of Mount Carmel, or Panagia Karmilou, *is* open. Inside, it's plain and simple, a stark contrast from many of the other churches we've visited, but it's no less beautiful for that.

It's the start of a Greek holiday weekend and the ferry from Piraeus has disgorged hundreds of Athenians escaping the city. Many have moved on to the resorts on the south and west coasts but Ermoupoli is still busy this evening. Well-dressed families walk up and down the harbour front. A Hell's Angels-type group of a dozen or so ageing motorcyclists rides slowly from one end of the seafront to the other, stops briefly, then rides back again. Young men cruise in open-topped cars. Teenage girls pretend they haven't noticed them. It's like no other Greek island we've ever visited and because it hasn't yet figured on the radars of the British package holiday companies it has very few non-Greek holidaymakers. For how much longer, we wonder. Given the ongoing economic instability, can they afford to continue to keep it to themselves?

*

A beautiful morning with a clear blue sky and no sign of the clouds that have been an almost permanent fixture during our time on Syros. We pack to the sound of the bells of half a dozen churches, then haul our bags down to Konstanza's office, half a floor below. Konstanza's not there – she's at church, apparently – but her daughter, a tall forty-ish woman with impossibly long legs and dyed auburn hair, runs our credit card through her machine, telephones for a taxi and presents us with a farewell gift of a box of loukoumi, the deliciously sticky Greek version of Turkish delight. A few minutes later we're in a queue at the port, waiting for Blue Star Lines' *Patmos* and ready to take our leave of Syros and the Cyclades.

PART TWO

Crete

Chapter One

Agios Nikolaos – No sign of Lady Gaga

We step out of Heraklion's Nikos Kazantzakis Airport into the sweltering early afternoon sun and cross the road to the little kiosk that describes itself rather grandly as the 'Bus Station'. We buy two one-way tickets at seven euros seventy each and within less than a quarter of an hour are on the KTEL bus heading towards Agios Nikolaos. Anyone who has ever travelled in Greece will know that every other small fishing boat and about every fifth village on the islands is called Agios Nikolaos, such is the nation's respect for its joint patron saint, but we're happy that we're heading for the right one, the one where we've booked our first few nights' accommodation on Crete. Equally, anyone who thinks that Crete is just another Greek island, albeit a very large island, is seriously mistaken. Cretans are proud and patriotic, Cretan before they are Greek, with their own distinctive culture and traditions. But as the bus makes its way east along the island's north coast, the traveller can be in no doubt that he or she is anywhere other than in Greece.

The road to Agios Nikolaos – sixty-one kilometres according to a road sign outside the airport – hugs the coast as it passes through the downmarket resorts of Hersonisos and Malia, chock-a-block with gaudy bars and tacky souvenir shops and barely clad sunburnt Brits of all ages and sizes. And then we cut across the pretty Cape Agios Ioannis and descend into Agios Nikolaos, reaching the town's bustling but slightly shabby bus station just after three. We've got a map of the town that we've downloaded from the internet and we've worked out that it's a walk of probably no more than five hundred metres to the Perla Apartments and Studios where we've booked a room. Once our bags have emerged from the bowels of the bus, we set off on foot.

We've been walking for about fifteen minutes when, away down a side street to our left, we catch a glimpse of the sea and what appears to be a beach. We know from its website that Perla overlooks a beach, so we head down the side street until we reach the seafront, confident that we're not far away. It's hot and we're a little sweaty, so we sit down outside a bar on the beach, order a beer each and try and work out exactly where we are and how close we are to the accommodation. After several minutes of searching and head-scratching, Barbara writes the name and address on a piece of paper and asks the waitress if she can point us in the right direction. The girl looks at the paper, frowns, then turns and takes it across the road into the bar, where we see her consulting with at least two other people. Eventually she emerges, puts the piece of paper back on the table and announces, "I'll phone for a taxi."

Agios Nikolaos is one of the largest towns on Crete and, having apparently set off from the bus station in totally the wrong direction, we're at the opposite end of it from where we want to be. We should have turned left out of the bus station, not right. Ten minutes and a five-euro taxi ride later, we're standing outside Perla being welcomed by our landlady. Popi Kaparaki is small, forty-ish and bubbly. She takes us up to our first-floor apartment, shows us where everything is, recommends several local places to eat, at least one of which just happens to be owned by one of her cousins, and gives us directions to the nearest supermarket. Perla does, as the website suggests, have "a seaview from the Gulf of Mirabello," but only if we sit sideways, one in front of the other, on the narrow balcony that hangs over a side street running at right angles to the bay.

The town is built around the little lagoon known as Voulismeni Lake, and its streets are lined with bars, tavernas and upmarket clothes shops. Local legend has it that the lagoon is bottomless, the crater of a long-extinct volcano. It was also rumoured locally that the Germans, when they were withdrawing from Crete in the Second World War, dumped their vehicles and weapons in the lake, although divers have investigated in recent years and as yet no evidence of this has been found. It's almost dark by the time we go out for dinner but Agios Nikolaos is alive with the twinkling lights of the cafés and restaurants. It's something of a poor man's Mykonos and, according to our guidebook, you can bump into an A-list celebrity at any time. "Think Cristiano Ronaldo, Leonardo DiCaprio and Lady Gaga," says the book. We do, but apart from one woman who looks vaguely like the brunette from Abba, we don't spot anyone famous. If they're here they're almost certainly tucked away in their fenced-off hillside villas or the smart hotels guarded by fierce-looking dogs further up the coast.

Swerving the taverna that's advertising "Rodsted lambstuffed" on its A-board, we have our first Cretan dinner at the somewhat bizarrely named Creta Embassy garden restaurant, where it's still just about warm enough to eat outside. The food is typically Cretan and excellent value, although the service is a little bit over-the-top and very Mykonos. Agios Nikolaos, on the other hand, is *not* typical Crete, but a Metaxa on the tiny balcony, watching the sparkling lights on the calm sea, puts to bed any thoughts I may have had that I won't like it.

*

The sun's shining and there's not a cloud in the azure sky when we venture out after breakfast. According to the BBC website, an Air Egypt plane on its way to Cairo with sixty-six people on board has gone missing not very far from where we are. It's later reported that debris has been found in the sea off Karpathos and it's almost certainly a terrorist attack. A couple of doors from Perla there's a classic case of Greek job creation going on where two young women armed with hosepipes seem to be washing the roof of a hotel that is currently being refurbished. Unlike Mykonos, which seems to exist to serve the needs of the young fashionistas, Agios Nikolaos is a real working town with a large street market running the length of one of its main thoroughfares, Paleologou Konstantinou. It's teeming with locals and tourists alike looking for an early-morning bargain. We hear French and Dutch being spoken, as well as what is probably Russian, but the only English we catch is when tourists of one of those nationalities need to communicate with the Greek stallholders. It's a wonderful atmosphere, the only disappointment being that the stall piled high with 'Ralph Lauren' polo shirts doesn't have a single one in my size.

Back down near our accommodation we get the bus to Elounda, a fishing village a dozen kilometres north of Agios Nikolaos from where we can get a little ferry to Spinalonga. The men who run these ferries had been making a modest living for years until, in 2005, Victoria Hislop published her novel *The Island*, which was based in Spinalonga and the little village of Plaka just to the north. Greek television pounced on it and produced a twenty-five-part drama series *To Nisi* ('The Island') in 2010, apparently the most expensive production in the history of Greek TV. As a result, tourism in this part of Crete went mad and everyone wanted to visit this tragic, haunted rock.

A barren islet covering eight and a half hectares, Spinalonga was once one of the most important defensive sea fortresses in the Mediterranean, built by the Venetians in the late sixteenth century. It was subsequently occupied by Turks and Muslims and by the late nineteenth century had more than eleven hundred inhabitants and twenty-five shops and workshops. In 1903 the Cretan state established a leper colony on the island, the first two hundred and fifty patients settling there the following year. The colony closed in 1973, and the islet remained desolate and uninhabited for many years, its use as a place of confinement and isolation having stigmatised it. Decent living conditions had in the 1950s and 1960s replaced the squalor in which many sufferers had lived, and Hislop's novel is woven around the story of an Athenian law student and leprosy sufferer who was largely responsible for introducing the changes.

It's busy, although not unbearably so today, and among the impressive and, in places, restored ruins there is plenty of shelter from the searing midday sun. It's hard to envisage what life might have been like for the poor souls who were exiled here – leprosy was after all a terrible but not very contagious disease. Hislop clearly felt what most people who visit Spinalonga feel, an overwhelming aura somehow left behind by those unfortunate people. It's a touching, almost heart-rending experience, but one that we would not have wanted to miss. And neither, presumably, would the German woman who sat in front of us on the ferry back to Elounda with her small sons Finley and Damian. We knew they were Finley and Damian from the tattoos on their mother's arms.

*

The bus from Agios Nikolaos to Kritsa deposits us at Melina Mercouri Square. An odd name, we think, for the area on the edge of a small Cretan village where the buses turn round, but we discover later that the actress and former Greek Culture Minister has history here. In the mid-1950s Mercouri and Jules Dassin chose Kritsa as the location for their film *The Greek Passion*. Many locals appeared as extras, as well as helping the film crew in other ways. Half a century before *The Island* gave tourism on Spinalonga and in Elounda a massive boost, *The Greek Passion* put Kritsa on many tourists' 'must visit' list and so grateful were the locals that they named a square after Mercouri. But we're not here to look for movie sets. We've got a kilometre walk down a hill from the village to see one of Crete's most remarkable churches.

The tiny, three-aisled church of Panagia Kera contains the finest Byzantine frescoes anywhere on the island. We pay our three-euro entry fee in the adjoining café and are immediately awestruck by the wall paintings, most of which date back to the early to mid-fourteenth century. A guide in Greece once told us that, in the time before most people could read, frescoes were a way of teaching the Bible. The dome and central nave of Panagia Kera are decorated with four gospel scenes – the Presentation, the Baptism, the raising of Lazarus and the entry into Jerusalem. Other walls portray the Crucifixion, the life of the Virgin Mary, the Second Coming, an enticing depiction of Paradise and a rather grim representation of the Punishment of the Damned, all beautifully restored and maintained.

Local tradition has it that the church also once contained an icon of the Virgin Mary said to have miraculous powers. It's not there anymore. It was removed and taken to Constantinople, only to be returned in 1498 and then, during the Venetian occupation of Crete, stolen again, this time by a Greek trader, and taken to the Temple of Saint Alonso in Rome.

We walk back up the hill into Kritsa and sit down for a well-deserved beer near a bust of another local heroine, Kritsotopoula. That wasn't her real name, for which I'm sure she was grateful. It means 'child of Kritsa'. She actually answered to Rhodanthe and she lived in the village in the early years of the nineteenth century during the Ottoman occupation. She's said to have stabbed an Ottoman soldier to death while he slept, then cut off her long hair and fled to the mountains disguised as a man to join the Cretan freedom fighters. It was only after she had been shot and mortally wounded in a battle with the Turks that her gender was revealed. She's everywhere in this pretty village, including in a bas-relief sculpture by an English artist that depicts her dying in the arms of her father, a local priest.

At the Taverna Platanos, halfway along the narrow street named after Kritsotopoula, we sit under a giant plane tree that the taverna owner tells us is over two hundred years old. Whether that's true or not, his moussaka is wonderful.

*

While we're having our last meal in Agios Nikolaos, at La Casa beside the lagoon, it begins to rain. It's the first rain we've had since we've been in Crete and it comes almost to the minute it's been forecast. We're undercover so it doesn't trouble us. In fact, we're only really aware of it from the effect of the raindrops falling on the lagoon. There are a couple of sharp showers and then it stops. As a result, it's fresher when we walk back to Perla after our meal, but it's still very warm, with no hint that the showers may have brought a permanent change in the weather. We stop at the bar below the Perla Apartments for a nightcap and get into conversation with the Dutch woman who's running it. She's interested in what we're doing and asks where we're heading next.

"You'll like Ierapetra," she says when we tell her, pronouncing it differently from the way we've been doing. But she has been on Crete for twenty-eight years, she tells us, so we guess she knows best. "I was there for a few years before I came to Agios Nikolaos. It's very nice, not so many tourists."

Chapter Two

Ierapetra – "Napoleon was here, possibly"

"Could you call a taxi to take us to the bus station, please?" we ask as we pay our bill at Perla.

"No need," says a smiling Popi. "My husband will take you. Just bring your bags downstairs."

Ten minutes later an old Skoda Fabia pulls up outside Perla's front door and the driver hops out, a small balding man who looks as if he could be Popi's father rather than her husband. He wedges the larger of our bags in the Skoda's boot, puts the other on the front passenger seat and motions us to get into the rear seats. He says nothing on the five-minute drive to the bus station, largely, we suspect, because he has only very limited English, but he does manage a "Goodbye and have a nice holiday," when he leaves us.

It's dull and overcast, the first morning since we've been on Crete that we haven't had sunshine and a clear blue sky, but it's still very warm. We buy our four euros ten cents tickets for the bus across the island to Ierapetra then find a seat outside. We have about twenty minutes to wait, time that will be spent in some rewarding people-watching. Among the other people waiting is one of the more interesting family groups we've seen recently. We first notice a couple, probably both aged around sixty, pushing two double buggies. In each buggy is a pair of identical and identically dressed twins, two girls in one buggy, two boys in the other, both pairs roughly the same age, almost certainly less than a year. From what we can hear of the conversation between the man and woman, we guess they're from somewhere in Scandinavia.

"Bit old to have children that young," we whisper. "And quads as well. Must have been on IVF."

Then two young men emerge from the bus station building. They're in their early thirties and quite obviously identical twins, although unlike the babies they're not dressed the same. Almost certainly the fathers of the twins in the buggies. And then two young women join the party, the partners of the young men and mothers of the babies – but, sadly, they're *not* twins. Probably not even sisters. But interesting, nevertheless. Of the ten people in the party, at least six are twins. What are the odds?

The bus trundles along the coast road for about twenty kilometres, the little twins playing happily on their parents' laps, until it reaches the village of Pachia Ammos, where there's a small holiday complex. At which point, the Scandinavian family gathers together buggies, bags and babies and leaves the bus. The bus then turns inland and heads through some fairly dull and uninteresting agricultural countryside until we emerge fifteen kilometres later at Ierapetra, on the island's south coast. The bus weaves its way through some narrow streets until it lands us at the bus station at around twelve-thirty. It's the usual Greek chaos, people trying to board the bus before the alighting passengers have had a chance to get off. Cars and motorbikes are parked on yellow lines, making it almost impossible for the bus driver to negotiate his way into his allotted spot. Elderly men are seated at tables outside the bus station café nursing ouzos and blocking the pavement.

The dull, overcast morning that we left behind in Agios Nikolaos has become a grey, threatening lunchtime. As we wheel our bags down the shopping street that will take us to our accommodation on the seafront, we become aware of a strong wind – becoming stronger the nearer we get to the sea. Painted in metre-high letters on a harbour wall, in English and Greek, is "Welcome to Europe's most southern town." Right now it doesn't feel that welcoming, nor particularly southern. On the seafront itself it's blowing a gale and the waves are lashing over the promenade. We've never seen the sea quite as wild in Greece. But at least it's not cold.

There's a broad pavement along the seafront, dividing the tavernas on the sea side and the souvenir shops on the town side. We find our accommodation, Katerina Rooms, up a steep narrow flight of stairs above one of the shops. We find Katerina herself in the shop below, and she takes the opportunity to show off some of the counterfeit designer clothes and genuine fridge magnets crammed into the shop before letting us into our rooms. The accommodation's modern, if a little minimal, and there's no kettle. But it's a great location overlooking the beach and the balcony will be a wonderful suntrap once the wind drops and the sky clears.

*

And by Sunday morning it has dropped. Not entirely, since from our balcony we can see that the sea is still being whipped up, but the sky's blue and cloudless. It takes an age to boil water in a saucepan for a cup of tea, a process that isn't helped by having the cold water tap fall into the sink, but we're eventually ready to go out and face the day. Ierapetra on a Sunday morning is a laid-back place to be. People are strolling up and down the seafront, the Promenade Markopoulou, enjoying a coffee outside one of the cafés or just sitting watching the sea as it continues to lash the harbour wall and enjoying the view of the mountains.

The most historically interesting aspect of the town ought to be Napoleon's House. The man himself is said to have stayed, incognito, with a local family one night in 1798 when he was on his way to Egypt. Even the family didn't appreciate who he was until he left the following morning to rejoin his ship anchored off the town and they found a note thanking them for their hospitality. Signed 'Napoleon Bonaparte' presumably, otherwise how would *anyone* have known? There's a sign on the seafront informing us that the house is 'fifty metres' down a little side street, a street that leads to the only house that it possibly could be. It's a two-storey, exposed stone corner house in desperate need of restoration. The wooden shutters are hanging off their hinges, the door, bearing the number nine, is firmly padlocked and there's no plaque or any other form of signage. But it has to be the right place because it *is* about fifty metres from the seafront and there's nowhere else in the vicinity that's anywhere near as old. The locals, so we've been told, are proud of the fact that Napoleon chose to stay there, but obviously not proud enough to make a fuss over the house he stayed in. And since there's no one around to talk about it, we take a couple of photographs and rather forlornly leave it behind.

The Venetian fortress, by contrast, has been impressively restored – and it's free to enter. Guarding the entrance to the harbour, it was built in the early years of Venetian rule of Crete and strengthened in the seventeenth century. It's an excellent place for clambering over and reading the information boards liberally scattered around the site, and the upper walls provide glorious views along the coast and up to the mountains. Just inland is the labyrinth that is the town's old quarter, full of old houses, two attractive churches, a Turkish fountain and a restored mosque with an imposing minaret. If only Napoleon's House had received the same attention.

Back on our balcony in the late afternoon we discover what a fair number of Cretans do in Ierapetra on a Sunday. Away to our left we can see part of what appears to be a municipal sports stadium. It's walled off and slightly shabby and comprises a four-lane running track around an overgrown grassy central area that is home to what looks like a long shed. But it's busy today with an assortment of joggers and walkers of all ages, shapes and sizes. Most are simply walking around the track, some on their own, others with one, two or more companions. Round and round they go, often apparently deep in conversation – with their fellow walkers or on their mobiles. It seems that Ierapetra is on a health kick, and the narrow streets aren't really suitable.

That they probably need to get out and walk somewhere in the fresh air is made clear to us in the evening. We'd planned to go to the highly recommended Napoleon taverna – "traditional Cretan… tasty dolmades, snails and spinach pies," says our guidebook – but having walked the length of the Promenade Markoupoulou we find it doesn't open on Sundays. So we walk back to Tzivarei, where we're the only customers apart from a table of twenty locals who appear to be celebrating something. Of the twenty, at least seventeen or eighteen are smoking, and one of those who isn't is a girl of about eleven or twelve. Food arrives at regular intervals throughout the evening and is devoured in between cigarettes. And all in a taverna which has a large sign on the wall that reads "In this shop smoking is not permitted".

It's still breezy as we walk back to the Katerina Rooms, but by no means as rough as when we arrived in Ierapetra thirty-six hours ago. According to the BBC Weather website we're set fair for the next ten days with temperatures heading into the mid-thirties. We're not just here for the good weather – but it helps!

*

The sea is flat calm, at least compared with the last couple of days, and it's warm, and sunny. People are walking and jogging around the running track and may have been all night for all we can tell. An elderly man just below our accommodation is fishing. The eleven o'clock excursion boat to the little island of Hryssi is loading its day-trippers. It leaves at six minutes past, punctual by Greek standards, the first time it has run since we've been here. It's a perfect day for just sitting on the balcony and watching the world go by.

When we do finally stir ourselves we make our way to the bus station and buy two return tickets to Myrtos, a pretty little village about fifteen kilometres along the coast. It's as noisy and chaotic as ever at the bus station. Elderly Greek women panic if there's any danger that they won't be first on the bus. The woman who sells tickets doubles up as the dispatcher and comes out of her office to supervise the comings and goings. It's all very confusing, but we do eventually get the right bus. Myrtos is the perfect antidote to the noise and bustle of Ierapetra on a weekday, a wonderfully relaxed hippyish village with a few narrow streets, a handful of shops and a sandy beach lined with tavernas and cafés. We have a drink and then lunch, washed down by some excellent local white wine, then amble back up to the main road to get the bus back to Ierapetra.

The joggers and walkers are still out in force as we get ready to go out. This time our walk along the seafront to the Napoleon taverna is rewarded. It's surprisingly quiet for somewhere that's supposed to be the best place in town to eat but the food is indeed very good and there's far more of it than we can handle. And with a litre of house red wine the bill comes to just twenty euros fifty, by far the cheapest dinner we've had since we've been on Crete. We've really come to like Ierapetra.

Chapter Three

Agia Galini – "It's €35 if you're German"

Given that there are virtually no roads along the south coast of Crete, getting to our next destination, Agia Galini, eighty kilometres to the west as the crow flies, is anything but easy. It means a three-hour bus journey to Heraklion, a trek across the city to its second bus station, then another two-hour journey back across the island to Agia Galini. There's the predictable chaos at the bus station, but we're in good time to buy our tickets to Heraklion on a bus that leaves precisely on time. There's a five-minute break in the bus station at Agios Nikolaos, enough to use the toilets and take on more passengers, and by the time we reach Heraklion's Bus Station A it's standing room only on the bus.

As we collect our bags from the bus's hold, we're approached by a man who appears to be organising the taxis.

"Where do you want to go?" he asks.

"Bus Station B."

"Special price, five euros," he says, grabbing the larger of our bags before we get a chance to answer and heading for the taxi at the front of the queue. We shrug our shoulders. We'd planned to walk, since according to our map it's less than a kilometre, but we have no choice. We climb into the back of the taxi and within three or four minutes we're being unloaded at Bus Station B. But at least it gives us plenty of time to buy our tickets for the next leg of the journey and enjoy delicious pita gyros in an adjoining café before our second bus is ready to leave.

It's a spectacular journey across the Nida Plateau, with Crete's highest mountain, the snow-capped Psiloritis, rising away to our right. The scenery is stunning, pretty little villages with main streets only just wide enough for our bus to pass through, hillsides dotted with tiny white churches. For reasons that are never explained, we stop in the little town of Mires, about fifteen kilometres short of our ultimate destination, where we have to change buses, but we still arrive in Agia Galini just before three.

We stand in what appears to be the centre of the village, houses and hotels clinging to the steep hillside, and wonder what to do next. As do another couple who've got off the bus with us. We've passed what we think is our accommodation, back up the hill, and don't relish the thought of hauling our bags up the road. The alternative seems to be a series of flights of steps, which will probably be even more difficult than the road. And as we weigh up our options we're approached by a tall, elderly Greek man who has an equally elderly Mercedes and who asks us where we want to go. He bundles all four of us, plus luggage, into his car and takes us on a ride that lasts less than a minute, charging us four euros for the privilege.

The Pallada, which we've pre-booked at thirty euros a night, is smart and modern with a sign above the front door that proudly announces the presence of a "fringe" in each room. It's also on top of the family-owned minimarket where our landlady Ioanna tells us we can get ten per cent discount off everything except stamps and cigarettes. Which is just as well. Her Metaxa is selling at nineteen euros a bottle compared with the twelve-seventy I paid at the Carrefour supermarket in Ierapetra. But it does mean that we won't have to carry groceries up the hill from the bottom of the village.

Running parallel to Agia Galini's main street are two narrower streets where most of the life seems to be. One is lined with souvenir shops and travel agencies and is known locally, and a little unimaginatively, as Shopping Street. The other, bursting with tavernas, is Food Street. We're spoiled for choice, and we have the added dilemma, since most of them have rooftop dining areas, of deciding whether to eat inside or out. In the end we choose inside at La Strada, which couldn't sound less Greek, but along with the pizzas serves some excellent local food. The swordfish steak and bifteki are superb.

There was a *Daily Mail* and a *Daily Mirror* on a newsstand when we arrived this afternoon, but by this evening they've gone. Which is strange. All we've heard since we've been here is German and Dutch, and the occasional French. So who's buying these English newspapers? Not that we would have done had they still been available.

*

Not discounting the fact that it's a charming and interesting village in itself, the main reason we're staying in Agia Galini is to visit the Minoan city of Phaestos and the caves at the hippy village of Matala. Having scrutinised the bus timetables last evening, we've come to the reluctant conclusion that the only practical way to do it is by hiring a car, so after breakfast, which has included some fresh-baked bread bought at the family shop below our room at Pallada, we set out to find the best deal among the half a dozen or so car rental agencies in the village. We're looking at the prices in the second one when we're approached again by the tall elderly man with the Mercedes.

"Where do you want to go?" he asks. We tell him. "I can take you," he responds.

"How much?" we ask.

"Are you German?"

"English."

"Twenty-five euros," he replies. And then after a short pause, "It's thirty-five if you're German."

We thank him for his kindness and decline. We like a bargain but we don't like that kind of prejudice. After checking all the agencies, we find a Fiat Panda at twenty-five euros for the day and book it for tomorrow morning. Most of the others were charging thirty to thirty-five, so we're pleased we shopped around.

Agia Galini claims to be the spot from where Icarus and Daedalus tried to escape from the Minoans by attaching home-made wings to their backs and attempting to fly to safety. Icarus didn't get too far, of course, plunging to his death after flying too close to the sun which melted the wax that was holding his wings together. The inventive Daedalus was said to have been more successful. There are statues of the two of them on a headland overlooking the harbour and in front of a small amphitheatre, which from what we can ascertain from an inscription was built as recently as 2013. One of the pair – we're not sure whether it's Icarus or Daedalus – has had part of one of his wings broken off. Nearby, the Agia Galini Museum of Folk Art, housed in what's known as Icarus's Cave but looks more like a garden shed, appears to be closed for good, which is a shame because it might have thrown some more light on this particular Greek myth. Like whether this *was* the actual spot from which they flew.

*

Next to our balcony at Pallada is a beautiful large hibiscus in full bloom. It attracts hundreds of bees and wasps, none of whom, thankfully, shows the slightest interest in us. We can have our breakfast in peace.

It takes us about an hour to reach Phaestos in our hired Panda. This is the second most important Minoan palace, after Knossos, built around two thousand BC and enjoying an awe-inspiring location with views over the Messara Plain and Mount Psiloritis. It would have been a formidable place in its day. It's quiet when we arrive and we're able to begin to enjoy the ruins virtually on our own. But it's not long before we hear French voices as two coachloads of visitors arrive, although to be fair they are as unobtrusive as two coachloads of French tourists can be. It's sad that many of the more interesting objects excavated at the site have been moved to the archaeological museum in Heraklion, as have many of the finds from Knossos. A small museum would add a great deal to the site.

We drive the eleven kilometres down to the coast and the village of Matala, which entered into Greek mythology as the place where Zeus, in the form of a bull, swam ashore with Europa on his back. The Minoans used it as the port for Phaestos and under Roman occupation it became the port for nearby Gortyna. Ruins of both ancient civilisations are still visible under the seabed, although what Matala means to most people these days is more to do with what happened there in the 1960s and 1970s than the mythology.

The village was home to a colony of hippies, some of them famous, like Joni Mitchell and Cat Stevens, who lived in the so-called caves. Ms Mitchell even referenced Matala in the song 'Carey' on her 1971 album *Blue*, and since that is one of my all-time favourite records, a visit to Matala is almost a pilgrimage. The 'caves' were in fact a Roman cemetery, not unlike the catacombs on Milos. Whatever artefacts were there were stolen or vandalised by the hippies, although in recent years the local authorities have taken steps to ensure that their historical significance is recognised. Unlike Joni and her friends, we have to pay three euros to scramble over the porous sandstone cliffs.

Matala's a pretty little village arranged around a horseshoe-shaped beach, not at all the pretentious, hippyfied place we'd been expecting. We're able to enjoy a drink and a reasonably priced lunch at one of the tavernas on the beach and I'm able to buy a Ralph Lauren baseball cap (genuine, no doubt!) at just five euros.

Back in Agia Galini we have our last meal at the Pantheon, one of the 'roof terrace' tavernas overlooking the harbour. We're surrounded by Germans, even our waiter speaks fluent German in addition to his excellent English, and we hope there aren't too many people here like the Mercedes owner just waiting to rip them off. This is a pretty, peaceful little village, nowhere near as spoiled as the guidebooks would have us believe, and we'll be a little sad to be leaving tomorrow. One thing is still worrying us, however. Just who did buy the last *Daily Mail*?

Chapter Four

Chora Sfakion – Slippery when wet

There appears to be a primary school up the hill by the side of our Agia Galini accommodation. Small children make their way up there this morning with varying degrees of enthusiasm – one boy of eight or nine wearing a Superman baseball cap and carrying a rucksack that's almost as big as himself seems particularly heavy-hearted. No doubt he'll be full of the joys of spring when he comes bounding back down the hill this afternoon.

Today we're facing our biggest challenge yet on Crete, our most complicated journey to date. Again, it's a relatively short distance along the coast as the crow flies to our next destination, Chora Sfakion, but today getting from A to B involves a detour via C and D. We've downloaded the KTEL bus timetables and are confident that it can be done, so after breakfast on the balcony spent watching the local children plodding up the hill to school we wheel our bags down the hill into the village and buy two single tickets for the next bus to Rethymno. We don't even respond to the Man with the Merc when he asks us where we're going, even though we're sure he would offer to do it for less, and in a shorter time, than the bus.

The first leg of the journey is a beautiful ride back over the island, through the pretty mountain village of Spili with its cobbled streets, flowered balconies and vine-covered rustic houses, until we reach the bus station in Rethymno on the north coast at about half past ten. We buy tickets to Vrysses, a village on the main road to Chania where we have to get our connecting service to Chora Sfakion, then wait rather nervously for a bus from Heraklion that, almost inevitably, is running late. But while they're rarely punctual, KTEL buses are generally reliable. At just after midday, along with a young Englishman who's travelling alone and like us heading for Chora Sfakion, we're deposited in the busy main street of Vrysses. In the café that doubles as the bus station, we buy our tickets for Chora Sfakion, accept the café owner's invitation to leave our bags in a corner and head outside to kill a couple of hours.

We settle down outside a taverna beside the little river that bisects the village and watch the ducks while enjoying a leisurely drink and a really good lunch. There's a free pudding and little individual bottles of raki thrown in at the end, but for once we don't touch the raki. Neither of us wants to sleep on the next leg of the journey. It's the most spectacular couple of hours' travelling we've had so far, across the Omalos Plateau with the towering Lefka Ori, or White Mountains, away to our right. It's a staggeringly beautiful, barren landscape and the journey ends with a breathtaking five kilometres of steep hairpin bends alongside the Imbros Gorge that lead down into the village of Chora Sfakion.

Cretan legend has it that the closer you get to Chora Sfakion the more bullet holes you see on the road signs. The area has long been known in Crete for its rebellious streak, particularly where foreigners are concerned. But we didn't need to worry. As we wheel our bags along the waterfront to the Lefka Ori taverna, at the end of a long row of cafés and restaurants, we're warmly greeted by all and sundry. At Lefka Ori, where we're staying for the next two nights, our landlord Andreas sits us down, gives us a cold beer each and tells us someone will be along in a minute to help us with our luggage.

Behind us as we sit enjoying our beer is a doorway and a steep flight of stairs. We assume that we're staying above the taverna and that Andreas thinks we're incapable of getting our bags up the stairs without assistance. But no. A man in his mid-twenties soon appears, probably Andreas's son. They exchange a few words before the young man approaches us, picks up the larger of our two bags, hoists it up onto his right shoulder and heads off, pulling the smaller bag behind him.

"Just follow him," Andreas tells us. It's a couple of hundred metres, up steps and a rough track, before we reach a smart new – no, not new, unfinished – apartment block. The young man unlocks one of the doors on a long corridor on a floor that *has* been completed, puts our bags just inside the door, smiles and heads back the way we've just come. We're in a brand new studio, everything clean and shining, but we'd have had a hard job finding it, and getting our bags up here, without help.

*

Pretty as it is, Chora Sfakion seems to exist only as the eastern terminus of the ferry service that runs along Crete's south-west coast. On the harbour there's a memorial commemorating the events of 1941 when thousands of British and ANZAC soldiers were evacuated from here following the Germans' successful invasion of the island. And in the nearby bus shelter there's a rather forlorn-looking British couple in their mid-fifties who are keen to talk to us.

"Can we get a taxi back to Chania from here?" asks the man. He has a strong Yorkshire accent.

"Not sure," I reply. "But you *can* get a bus."

He shakes his head. "We've missed it. We've missed the last one."

We're baffled. According to the timetables we've downloaded, and the small printed notice on the bus shelter wall, the last bus from Chora Sfakion to Chania is at six-thirty, just after the ferry from Agia Roumeli arrives. It's currently just after half past five. "You've got plenty of time," I tell them. "Almost an hour."

"But it's half past seven," he says. "The last bus went over an hour ago."

By now a young Greek man has joined us. "What time is it?" I ask him. He's heard some of the conversation and is as baffled as we are.

He looks at his phone. "Five-thirty."

"That's what my watch says," I add.

The Yorkshireman and his wife are now almost speechless and totally confused. He takes his smartphone from a pocket and shows us the screen. The figures 19.35 are clearly displayed.

"We bought this last week, before we came out here," he says. "We thought we wouldn't need to bother with watches. I put it forward two hours when we were on the flight over so it should…"

"You put it forward manually?" I interrupt, the penny having dropped. "You didn't need to do that. These things normally tend to adjust themselves automatically as you change time zones. You've been four hours ahead of UK time instead of two ever since you arrived."

He has difficulty hiding his embarrassment but does his best to make light of it. "No wonder there was no one around when we went down for breakfast at eight this morning!"

We can't help feeling sorry for them, but when they tell us what they've been doing our pity turns to admiration. They're serious walkers and a couple of days ago did the descent of the legendary Samaria Gorge. But instead of following tradition and getting a ferry from the foot of the gorge and a coach back to Chania, they've spent two days walking along the rugged, inhospitable south coast, staying overnight at a halfway point and reaching Chora Sfakion just over an hour ago.

We wish them well as we wander back down to the waterfront, but I can't resist adding, "You can get a watch in Chania for five euros, you know." They smile and then settle down on the bus shelter bench to wait for the ferry to come in and the connecting bus to arrive, somewhat happier than they were five minutes ago.

*

It's quiet, almost too quiet, the next morning. For the first time since we arrived on Crete there's barely a breath of wind, there's no traffic anywhere near our accommodation, no children on their noisy way to school. The only sound is that of the odd dog barking somewhere in the distance. It's a beautiful day with a temperature of around thirty degrees and we decide to do very little. Down at the little port we buy our tickets for tomorrow's ferry to Paleochora, watch transfixed for about fifteen minutes as a local bus makes its way up a series of hairpin bends on a newly constructed road on one of the hills behind the harbour and then disappears in the direction of the mountain hamlet of Agios Ionannis, then settle down outside a café for the first cold beer of the day.

It's very warm and very relaxed and if you stayed here more than a couple of days you might just get bored. But Chora Sfakion is the perfect place to unwind and it's one of the friendliest communities we've ever encountered. It's also the scene of our, or at least *my*, first minor mishap.

The walls and floor in the bathroom of our smart new studio are covered in gleaming ceramic tiles, so highly polished and shining there's barely a need for a mirror. Unfortunately, when they're wet they're also extremely slippery and there *is* a need for a bath mat. And because they shine so brightly water on them doesn't show up. As I enter the bathroom just after Barbara has had her early evening shower my left foot skids across the floor. I know I'm going to fall but there's nothing I can do to prevent it. It's like one of those slow-motion experiences. Various parts of my anatomy come into contact with various hard surfaces as I crumple to the floor. I'm not sure what kind of noise I've unwittingly emitted, some sort of profanity no doubt, but Barbara has clearly heard it.

"Are you all right?" she calls, although if I'm honest she doesn't sound as concerned as I think she ought to be.

I lie still for a second or two until I'm sure that there's nothing broken, or even too badly bruised, other than my dignity, then reply in what I hope is a suitably pathetic tone, "I'm fine."

And as far as I can tell, I am. I slowly haul myself back onto my feet and all I can feel is a little soreness in my left hip. There'll be a few bruises in the morning, no doubt.

At midnight, when everything in this lovely little village has long been closed for the night, I sit on my balcony with a Metaxa and muse over the fact that we are now roughly halfway through our tour of Crete. It's all gone remarkably well so far. The buses have been where we want them to be more or less *when* we want them. The accommodation has been excellent, the villages we've stayed in beautiful and friendly. And tomorrow we move on again. Barbara has received an email from the owner of the apartment we've booked in Paleochora telling us that we will be welcomed "by Vasilis with Joy". Vasilis is our landlord. No doubt we'll find out who Joy is when we arrive.

CHAPTER FIVE

Agia Roumeli – "It's very old"

There's been a slight change in the weather. It's still very warm, but there's a good deal of cloud and more wind than we've become used to. Surprisingly, I'm not too bruised after my bathroom mishap. A little stiff in one or two of my joints but considering the impact with which I hit the floor, not too bad at all. We manage to get our luggage down the steps and the rough track and back to the waterfront and sit outside the Samaria Bar to enjoy a last drink and wait for the ferry. The *Samaria I* arrives on the horizon pretty much on time, and so we say goodbye to some of the many friendly people we've talked to since we've been in Chora Sfakion and make our way to the boarding point.

The ferry heads westward, hugging the coast until it reaches the tiny and very pretty fishing village of Loutro, where we spent an hour or so when we were on Crete six or seven years ago. It's a quiet arc of flower-covered blue-and-white buildings lining a narrow stony beach and the only way to reach it is on foot or by boat. Surprisingly, since it's so small, it's the only natural harbour on the entire south coast of Crete. It was once a strategically important port and St Peter is said to have set off on one of his journeys from here. Today, it's just a base for walkers or for those who want to do nothing more than chill out on the beach.

We leave Loutro and cruise along the rugged, dramatic coastline to Agia Roumeli, the coastal village that seems to exist only to serve the needs of the hikers exiting the Samaria Gorge. Europe's most famous gorge is, apparently, a 'must do' experience for visitors to Crete – younger and fitter visitors than us, anyway – and at times like this can see as many as three thousand walkers a day negotiating its rocky, sixteen-kilometre route. Agia Roumeli isn't much of a village and it's not much to look at either, but it must seem like paradise to the footsore thousands. There's a sizeable collection of tavernas and bars, not to mention the souvenir shops selling 'I survived the Samaria Gorge' tee-shirts, all of which do a steady trade as the day progresses and the walkers emerge from the gorge.

If you take this ferry westwards from Chora Sfakion and Loutro, you have no choice but to spend three or four hours in Agia Roumeli, since it ties up at the little jetty and waits for those who have completed the gorge walk. What happens to walkers who finish the trek after five-thirty, when the ferries to the east and west both leave, is anyone's guess, since the ferries are the only way out. It's a little like Dunkirk in 1940 – without the bullets and bombs, of course. But at least we're allowed to leave our bags on board *Samaria I* and we step off the boat and look for somewhere to have lunch and a drink.

A taverna called Parra has a balcony where we can sit and watch the steady trickle of walkers as they complete their walk through the gorge. They come in twos and threes, in all shapes and sizes, all ages although mostly under fifty, and all nationalities. Some look completely knackered, their legs unsteady, their feet clearly sore; others look so fresh they could probably turn round and do it all again. Many walk straight across the beach and into the sea, without taking off their boots. But most look happy, wearing satisfied and elated expressions like the finishers in a big city marathon.

After lunch we wander around the village and walk up towards the end of the gorge – the only people heading in that direction. It's quiet and much less commercial away from the beach area, where the tavernas and bars fill up as the afternoon wears on. Returning, we settle down at a bar for another drink and to kill some time until we can board the ferry again.

Agia Roumeli is hemmed in by tall hills and on one, about a kilometre out of the village, are the ruins of a Venetian castle. It clearly intrigues one walker, a man in his forties who, from his accent, is probably German or Scandinavian. He approaches the counter of the bar where we're seated and asks the young woman serving, while gesturing towards the ruins, "What's that place?"

She turns to an elderly man behind her who's making coffee and speaks to him in Greek. "Kastell," we hear him say. "He says it's a castle," she tells the tourist.

The visitor smiles. "How old is it?" he asks. The young woman again turns to her elderly colleague and, presumably, repeats the question. He again mutters something in reply.

"He says it's very old." The younger man thinks about asking something else, then decides not to and walks away, a slightly baffled expression on his face.

At just after five, *Samaria I* and its sister ship which is heading back towards Loutro and Chora Sfakion lower their ramps and allow people to start boarding. The tavernas and cafés empty rapidly as hundreds of people scramble to get a decent seat. The ferry on which we had been two of only about twenty passengers when it left Chora Sfakion earlier, is now packed. Since we've stored our bags down on the car deck, we can mingle with the other passengers looking as if we've walked the gorge as well. Unless they look at our feet, that is. We're virtually the only people on board not wearing dust-covered walking shoes or shoeless and nursing blisters – as well as being considerably less red-faced than most.

Three-quarters of an hour on, we reach the village of Sougia, another village that owes much to its proximity to the Samaria Gorge, although it does have some remains of Roman and Byzantine occupations. Not that any of our fellow passengers linger long enough to visit any of them. A short distance away from the jetty where *Samaria I* stops is a line of coaches all pointing out of the village. Many of the hundreds who piled onto the ferry at Agia Roumeli now stream off and head for the coaches, ready to be transferred to various parts of the island, no doubt sleeping most of the way. We watch them go, then spend another three-quarters of an hour cruising westward beneath dramatic cliffs on a mill-pond calm sea until, bathed in the soft pink light of the setting sun, we reach our next destination, Paleochora, at just after seven.

CHAPTER SIX

Paleochora – 'Don't worry – be happy'

We came to Paleochora once before, six years ago, and had been looking forward to this stage on our Cretan travels probably more than any other. 'Pally', as it's familiarly known to those who visit often, is the largest settlement in this corner of Crete. The resident population is little more than fifteen hundred but the town punches above its weight, a seemingly impossible combination of the lively and the laid-back, and we remember it as somewhere you can do as little or as much as you want. It all looks very familiar as we haul our bags from the quay to our accommodation. We find Koxyli Studios in a slightly scruffy back street, a smart, well-equipped complex only a couple of minutes' walk from one of Paleochora's two beaches and a large, well-equipped and relatively cheap supermarket. And Vasili, a small, smiling man of about seventy, is there to greet us as promised – although there's no sign of Joy!

Those who know Paleochora, and that includes my sister Lynda and her husband who come here every year, recommend eating at Captain Dimitrios, a taverna on the stony beach. It has, by all accounts, the best house red wine in town, so we decide to have our first dinner there. It's a little disconcerting when we go out and discover that none of the town's street lights are working, although because it's not yet fully dark and many of the shops are still illuminated and open we don't have too much trouble finding our way. But is this another sign of austerity biting? Does the local council not have the money to switch the lights on?

The red wine at Captain Dimitrios is indeed very good, so good that we share a litre of it. And the food is pretty decent, too, and relatively inexpensive. But getting back to Koxyli Studios with only the stars to light our way is somewhat less enjoyable. We get hopelessly lost in the pitch-black streets until we find ourselves on the road that runs along the town's sandy beach. We turn back on ourselves and head down what we think is a side street that should lead to Koxyli – then double back the instant we're approached by what in the dark looks like a ferocious German Shepherd on a long chain. When we do eventually make it back to the studio we haven't a clue where we've been, but we're surprised to find we've got mud on our shoes.

*

We can't stay on the south coast of Crete without doing a gorge walk, even though we have no intention of attempting the Samaria. But there's one we've heard of just a few kilometres outside Paleochora, and after a good night's sleep and an energy-giving breakfast (boiled eggs and soldiers) we set off to tackle it. To get to the start we need to walk up to the little mountain village of Anydri, five kilometres away via a winding road with no bus service. It's obviously uphill all the way once we get to the outskirts of the town but it's a relatively gentle incline and much of it is in the shade of tall cliffs. Goats wander in the bushes on either side of the road, the occasional farmer is working in the nearby fields, and every now and again a car passes us whose driver gives us a rather bewildered look.

It takes us about an hour and a quarter to reach Anydri, where we stop at To Skolio ('The School'), a converted schoolhouse with a courtyard overlooking a wooded gorge and the Libyan Sea in the distance. No sooner are we seated than a young woman brings us a jug of iced water and takes our drinks order. We've got other things to do, but we're in no hurry to leave the village. Just below To Skolio's terrace is the tiny church of Agios Georgios, renowned for its fourteenth-century frescoes. They are indeed impressive, although in urgent need of restoration, and portray St George slaying the dragon and other scenes. We're not sure what the connection is between Crete and St George, despite the numerous churches, villages and fishing boats dedicated to the saint and the celebrations on 23rd April, but it's very strong. The little churchyard contains about twenty graves, most of them, surprisingly, bearing the same surname. It's a monument to the aforementioned rebellious nature of the Sfakion region. The founding fathers of Anydri were two brothers who fled from a vendetta and now most of the villagers have their surname.

We enjoy a long leisurely lunch back at To Skolio and as a result are almost reluctant to tackle the gorge. We half-contemplate taking the road back down to Paleochora, but give ourselves a mental rap over the knuckles and set off down the track beside the church. The first few hundred metres are relatively easy going down a well-worn path. But it becomes increasingly difficult as we descend and in places the path, which follows the dried-up bed of a stream, is almost completely overgrown. High above us large birds of prey (vultures?) circle in the clear blue sky and there's very little shelter from the early afternoon sun. In my head I can hear Frankie Laine singing 'Cool Water'. "All day I face the barren waste…"

We walk, scramble and even shuffle on our backsides for about half an hour until we reach what appears to be an impossible obstacle. It's a sheer drop down a rock face of about three metres, at one side of which someone has attached a rope to the trunk of a tree, presumably providing a means of descending. Neither of us fancies the rope. We look back, think about returning to Anydri, then rule that out as well. Neither of us fancies going back up the hill either. We walk back and forth across this little clifftop until, on the opposite side to the rope, I spot a possible way down. There's a bush growing out of the rock, its strong-looking branches suddenly looking to me like a ladder. I clamber down it, facing the rock face, until I feel *terra firma* beneath my feet and then persuade Barbara to do the same. Our legs are covered in scratches but at least we're down – and the vultures are no longer circling.

Cleaned up and refreshed from our bottles of water, we have another hour of energetic walking and scrambling until we emerge onto the Gialiskari Beach, where an enterprising local has set up a cantina and we're able to reward ourselves with ice creams and a couple of cold beers. The last part of the journey is along the E4 European walking route that starts in Portugal and ends in Kissamos, in Crete's north-western corner. It's well-maintained and relatively flat and gets us back into Paleochora at around five-thirty. We've walked and scrambled around fifteen kilometres, enjoyed an excellent lunch and seen some interesting and spectacular sights. A very good day.

*

Since we arrived in Paleochora we've seen small posters stuck to lamp posts and telegraph poles all over the town advertising "Traditional Greek music – live" at the Samaria taverna. We know the place from when we've been here before, an interesting taverna in a partly derelict house serving very good food. After a couple of hours' rest following our day's exertions, a shower and a change of clothes, we set off – and most of the street lights seem to be working again.

We enter the taverna to the sound of Bob Dylan's 'Knocking on Heaven's Door'. Two middle-aged men are seated on high stools, strumming guitars. They go on through a repertoire that includes 'Mrs Robinson', 'Don't Worry – Be Happy' and 'Living Next Door to Alice' before taking a break. When they return to their stools after about fifteen minutes they *do* play some vaguely Greek material, although not very traditional and nothing more adventurous than 'Zorba's Dance' and the theme from *Never on Sunday*, before returning to a mixture of Western rock and pop. Still, the food's very good and it *is* a very entertaining evening.

*

Another beautiful morning in Paleochora and after the exertions of yesterday we take our time getting going. When we do eventually walk into the village centre we're slightly seduced by the posters outside the travel agencies advertising "Dolphin spoting (*sic*) excursions," so we shell out seventeen euros each for the trip that leaves at five o'clock this afternoon then head for a beach-front bar and our first refreshments of the day.

It's a little later in the morning, as we rediscover this lovely town, that we find ourselves in the little cemetery and come across something that isn't mentioned in any guidebooks or on any local websites. In one corner of the cemetery is what appears to be a mass grave, the final resting place of thirty-two men, all of whom had died in 1941. According to the headstone their ages ranged from seventeen to sixty-five and our basic understanding of the Greek alphabet enables us to identify at least two pairs of brothers and one father and son. Not very far away, on the road out of the village towards Chania, stands a simple, and, sad to say, somewhat neglected memorial. We stand in silence for some minutes, believing that something awful must have happened here but not knowing what.

We've borrowed a little locally published booklet that had been in the reception area at Koxyli and over lunch we uncover the sad story behind the grave and the memorial. After their invasion and the short-lived Battle of Crete in 1941, the Germans swept through this part of the island, arresting and generally executing any Cretans they believed had resisted them or helped Allied soldiers escape. In this case they had picked up twenty-nine men from Paleochora and the surrounding villages and held them in a makeshift jail that had been the local police station. They were never properly tried. Each morning over a period of two or three weeks all of them were marched out to the spot where the memorial now stands and three or four were executed by firing squad. The remaining men were then ordered to bury their dead compatriots in the cemetery before being marched back to the prison to spend the subsequent twenty-four hours wondering which of them would be next. Three other men who had been killed in their vain attempt to defend their island were buried alongside them.

It explains, though doesn't totally justify, the attitude of the man with the Mercedes in Agia Galini. Seventy-five years on it's still a deeply disturbing period of our history and it seems that Cretans have very long memories.

*

It's a beautiful calm late afternoon when we take our place in the queue on the quayside for the dolphin-spotting cruise. While the operators are quick to point out that there's no guarantee of seeing any of these wonderful creatures, they do advertise the odds as "seventy per cent." Sadly, this evening we appear to be in the other thirty per cent. We head out of Paleochora in the direction of the island of Gavdos, the most southerly point in Europe, sixty kilometres away but clearly visible on an evening like this. One member of the boat's two-man crew, a middle-aged man, stands in the bow of the boat, his eyes intensely scanning the expanse of still, dark blue water that surrounds us.

We turn east and head towards Sougia and Agia Roumeli, first hugging the coastline beneath the cliffs, then cruising away from the land. We take photographs of a spectacular sunset as we sail west back towards Paleochora, we strain our eyes trying to detect tell-tale signs of dolphin activity on the surface. But dolphins we don't see. We should have been warned. Despite the seventy per cent odds advertised by the travel agents, the local tourism guide states simply "*with any luck* some of these wonderful creatures can be seen close at hand." We *are* however treated to an acrobatic display by a shoal of flying fish. Like silver bats they shoot out of the sea, skim just above the surface in a thirty- or forty-yard arc then dive back into the depths. A magical sight that almost makes up for the lack of dolphins.

After dinner – the street lights came on before eight o'clock this evening, while it was still broad daylight – we're enjoying a drink outside the Cosmogonia café at the crossroads in the centre of the village when my mobile phone buzzes. It's my sister and long-time 'Pally' fan who's suggesting we stand in front of the webcam above the crossroads and wave to them. It's largely at the instigation of her son, who's with them at the moment and they're looking at pictures from the webcam on his laptop. He's apparently suggested that we might moon for the camera, but his mother's drawn the line. We do, however, take it in turns to stand in front of the pharmacy at the crossroads and wave at the camera high above the street. We get text confirmation that they can see us on the laptop and are waving back – and a text message with which we can't disagree saying simply "How sad?"

*

This morning we walk along the road next to the sandy beach, passing the slightly incongruous metal sculpture of Laurel and Hardy and a donkey, until we reach the Zygos taverna, known in this part of Crete for its excellent breakfasts. It's another beautiful day, although there's a strong wind blowing on this side of the peninsula, but Zygos has sufficient protection to enable us to sit on its patio, and while we enjoy delicious omelettes and fresh orange juice we are unwittingly entertained by Paleochora's answer to Trigger from *Only Fools and Horses*.

A small man, probably aged around fifty, his role in life seems to be keeping the kerbsides clear of sand and cigarette butts, and on his pushcart he has a broom, a dustpan with a long handle and a seemingly infinite supply of black plastic sacks. He makes slow progress, partly because the sacks are too heavy to lift once he's shovelled in about three pans of sand, so he continually has to replace them, and partly because the fact that he's next to the beach means that more sand blows back into the kerb almost as soon as he's swept it up. We probably stay outside the taverna for about three-quarters of an hour and he covers no more than twenty metres of kerb.

At the end of the peninsula there's a thirteenth-century Venetian castle, the Castello Selino, built so the occupiers could survey Crete's south-western coast from a commanding position. Our guidebook tells us it's worth clambering up among the ruins to admire the view, and so we do. There isn't much left. It's been destroyed by invaders several times, the last occasion being by the Germans during the Second World War.

According to the information boards, several hundred thousand euros have been spent on renovations, mostly thanks to the European Union, with the usual Greek disregard for health and safety regulations. There's no sign of a fence or a handrail and there are opportunities everywhere for tripping or falling down steep drops.

But it does give us a clear view of Paleochora's port and marina, excluding Heraklion and Chania probably the largest on the island. It was developed in the 1980s, again with EU millions, but apart from half a dozen little fishing boats it's unused. It was intended to relieve pressure on the two main ports on the north coast but the infrastructure to accompany it, like a road that doesn't run right through the middle of the town, has never been built, making it impossible for trucks to get in and out. And the way things stand in Greece at the moment, it will be a long time before that happens.

Back down at sea level we pay a couple of euros each to visit the curiously named Museum of the Acritans of Europe. It's more of a permanent exhibition than a museum and has a fine collection of musical instruments, weapons and other artefacts from medieval and Byzantine times. We're not sure what an Acritan is or was, but the museum appears to be dedicated to the fighters and heroes of those eras – there are no English translations – and names like St George, Alexander the Great and El Cid all feature. It's a little baffling, but we enjoy it.

We're having an after-dinner drink outside Cosmogonia later when we meet Trevor and Julie, a couple of about the same age as us from Nottingham who are here for a fortnight and who we chatted to a couple of nights ago.

"How's your day been?" I ask once we're all settled with our drinks.

"Great," says Trevor. "We've been dolphin-spotting this evening."

"Any good?" I'm expecting, if not hoping for, a response that will indicate they've had an experience similar to ours.

"Not half," Trevor replies. "It was brilliant. We practically had to fight them off, there were so many. They were trying to jump into the boat."

"Great," I say through gritted teeth, then quickly change the subject.

Chapter Seven

Chania – Cat on a hot car bonnet

There was a wedding yesterday evening, a truly unique Greek celebration. Somewhere in the distance we'd heard the motorcade as it toured this little town, horns blaring, everyone's peace shattered. As we fell asleep we were aware of the occasional burst of gunfire and the music – real Greek music this time. Now, as we pull our bags through the narrow streets, it's hard to avoid the spent shotgun cartridges that are almost everywhere. How no one ever gets hurt at a Greek wedding is something of a miracle. Or we assume no one ever gets hurt. You never hear if they do.

The bus to Chania leaves from outside a café – known as the bus station – on the road leading out of Paleochora at just after midday. There are about a dozen of us on board, ourselves, a Scandinavian family of mother, father and two small boys and a handful of locals. We climb steadily up into the mountains until, after half an hour and about twenty kilometres, we reach Kandanos, arguably the best known of Crete's Martyred Villages. In June 1941 the village was completely destroyed and a hundred and eighty of its inhabitants killed by the Germans in a reprisal for the participation of local people in the Battle of Crete. They had held up the German advance to the south of the island for two days.

Nearby villages suffered a similar fate but none on such a scale as Kandanos, whose buildings were ruthlessly torched by the invaders. The village was completely rebuilt after the war and memorials now honour the dead, both the hundred and eighty locals and the twenty-five German soldiers who lost their lives in the conflict in the area. Today, as we stop briefly to pick up a couple of passengers, we notice men in traditional Cretan dress – wide breeches tucked into knee-length boots – and buildings decked with bunting. Kandanos is marking the anniversary of the atrocity.

We travel across the ruggedly beautiful backbone of the island, through several more Martyred Villages, until we reach the north coast near Maleme, site of a cemetery containing the graves of over four thousand German soldiers. Ironically, one of those who once cared for the graves here was George Psychoundakis, a resistance fighter who for a period of about two years during the occupation was a dispatch runner for the young British officer Patrick Leigh Fermor and the undercover troops who remained on the island. His memoir of the occupation was published in 1955 as *The Cretan Runner* and turned into a film a year later as *Ill Met by Moonlight*.

We head due east on the gaudy, twenty-kilometre coastal strip – all-inclusive hotels and elaborate crazy golf courses lining both sides of the road, perhaps Crete's least attractive area – until we reach the central bus station in Chania a few minutes after two o'clock. It's a hot, sticky afternoon and Chania is noisy and dirty but it takes us no more than ten minutes to find our accommodation. Stoa Rooms is in Lithinon Street, just one block back from the old Venetian harbour in one of the town's most picturesque districts. We're warmly welcomed by Konstantine, a tall good-looking young man in his middle twenties who gives us iced tea and chocolate biscuits, and when we compliment him on his excellent English he tells us that his late mother was from Liverpool and he was brought up in a bilingual home.

Chania on a Friday evening is lively and noisy, and the tavernas and bars around the harbour are inevitably busy. And they're as expensive as anywhere we've seen since we left Agios Nikolaos. We wander the back streets away from the waterfront until we reach a narrow, pedestrianised lane lined with restaurants and bars that are considerably cheaper. We settle down at a table outside the almost unpronounceable Oinopoieio, which we gather means the Winery, and enjoy a really good meal and a bottle of house red wine for less than thirty euros, then treat ourselves to a nightcap in the comfort of the padded chairs of a café overlooking the harbour.

As we enjoy our drinks, a swarthy skinny man who is probably in his mid-thirties with long unkempt hair, an untidy beard and shabby black clothes shuffles towards where we're sitting, seemingly barely able to walk. He eventually stands by our table bent and mumbling incomprehensibly, his left hand outstretched, palm upturned. We try hard not to make eye contact as his voice becomes weaker and weaker, then breaks as he appears to begin crying. We have no idea what he's saying or what he wants, other than money, but a Greek family at the next table – man, woman and boy of seven or eight – take pity on him and give him money. He nods his thanks and shuffles slowly away, then, when he thinks no one is watching, he straightens up and breaks into a brisk walk. He heads for a kiosk on the street corner where he buys a can of Mythos lager and walks swiftly away.

*

The Maritime Museum of Crete, part of the formidable Venetian-built Firkas Fortress, stands at the western entrance to the harbour and is an impressive celebration of the island's nautical history and tradition. It's more than worth the three-euro entrance fee and for more than two hours we're absorbed by its massive collection of model ships, naval instruments, photographs, paintings and other memorabilia. A whole section is devoted to Crete's many naval battles and on the first floor the Second World War gets suitably in-depth coverage.

A couple of hundred metres behind the Mosque of Kioutsouk Hasan, and just off the harbour, we find Doloma, a little family-run highly-recommended taverna where we're invited into the kitchen to choose our lunch rather than being given a menu and then settle down on the outdoor terrace. There's a sort of yard in front of us that's being used as a parking lot by several locals and as somewhere shady to sleep by several cats, but despite a plethora of comfortable-looking spots one feline seems desperate to make life difficult for itself. He or she decides that the narrow, steeply sloping bonnet of an old Renault van will make the ideal bed. We watch as the cat curls itself up as close to the windscreen as possible, then closes its eyes. Slowly, inevitably, it begins to slide down the bonnet, waking with a start and realising what's happening. It lashes out in a desperate attempt to grab the windscreen wipers with its claws but fails miserably – and lands in a heap on the gravel. It shakes its head and for a split second looks mildly embarrassed. Then, like all cats would, it springs up, gives us a look that says 'I meant to do that' and leaps back up onto the Renault's bonnet. Within less than a minute the process is repeating itself, but the cat still hasn't learned. Only after crashing to the ground for the third time does it lick its wounds and wander somewhat sheepishly away to a dark corner of the square. The pre-lunch entertainment is excelled only by lunch itself.

We've been told by the man running Doloma that we can get a bus to the Souda Bay War Cemetery from outside a nearby supermarket. The number thirteen runs every twenty minutes, he tells us, and it goes right past the cemetery. He's right on the first part, the number thirteen does indeed pick up outside the supermarket three times an hour, but wrong on the second. We're still on the bus when it reaches its final destination, a naval hospital on the far side of the little town of Souda. Through a fellow passenger, a young Greek man who speaks English, we manage to tell the driver what we're trying to do and he agrees to let us stay on the bus as it turns round and heads back to Chania, and to drop us off at the point on its route nearest to the cemetery.

The driver's as good as his word. Back on the other side of Souda he stops at a crossroads, points up a road signposted for Chania Airport and says in his best English, "One kilometre." We thank him and set off under a burning sun in the direction he's indicated. He's been somewhat generous in his estimation of the distance. It's a good half-hour walk along a busy-ish road, but eventually we get there. Here, in a tranquil location at the edge of Souda Bay, are the graves of fourteen hundred British, Australian and New Zealand soldiers and airmen who lost their lives in the Battle of Crete. Like the cemeteries of Northern France and Belgium, it's quiet and beautifully cared-for. There is a handful of other visitors but barely a sound. A truly moving experience.

After paying our respects we buy a bottle of water at a nearby kiosk and walk back into Souda to wait for the next bus back to Chania.

*

Crete's second-largest settlement, Chania is a city of contrasts, somewhere that you become acutely aware of the economic crisis that is still gripping Greece, of the gulf between the haves and the have nots. On our way out of Stoa Rooms to undertake a walking tour of the picturesque Venetian quarter we bump into our landlord Yiannis. He's a big, well-dressed man in late middle age who clearly has investments other than these studios. He's polite but almost formal as he asks if everything is up to our expectations, and when he's satisfied that we're happy he goes to a cupboard and fishes out a bottle of red wine for us, a bottle that bears his own label. And then disappears into his office.

At the new harbour at lunchtime we watch children in their identical smart designer sailing gear messing about in boats, little sailing dinghies at the Chania Sailing Club. Small children whose parents drive along the quayside in their Mercedes and BMWs and drop them off or pick them up again. Meanwhile, unwashed youngsters of the same age, scruffily clothed and some of them in bare feet, wander among the taverna tables with battered accordions they can't play, begging from the tourists. On the smaller islands and in the inland villages, where the local economy is largely cash, such scenes are rare, but here in Chania there are an awful lot of people, particularly young adults, who don't seem to do very much. And many of those working in the bars and tavernas and in the tourist shops are almost certainly working for cash in hand, we've been told. Taking the tourists' euros but not paying tax – the Greek malaise.

Chapter Eight

Georgioupoli – The dearest beer on Crete

We're on the road again this morning, although only as far as Georgioupoli, a village whose name only the locals can pronounce, thirty kilometres east of Chania. We haul our bags up the half-kilometre or so to the KTEL bus station, buy our tickets, then sit and enjoy a coffee until the bus driver decides it's time to move. And then he takes us almost by surprise. We hadn't realised beforehand but Georgioupoli is the first stop on the express bus service route to Heraklion and we're on its outskirts almost before we realise.

The bus driver deposits us on the main road, helps us get our bags from the luggage hold, wishes us well and disappears into the distance. We cross the road and head down a narrowish lane, assuming correctly that it will take us into the village. It's four or five hundred metres down to the spacious square, where we stop and try to get our bearings. We've printed off a map but we still can't really work out where we're supposed to go. And then, quite by chance, about thirty metres down one of the side streets we spot a sign hanging off a building – Zorba's, the accommodation we've booked online.

There's an unstaffed reception area which reminds us of a Travelodge, bare and not very welcoming. We ring the bell on the counter and wait until a girl of about twelve or thirteen appears. She smiles politely but doesn't really understand what we want. She goes away again and we wait a little longer until a middle-aged woman arrives. She *does* understand us, and after taking an imprint of Barbara's credit card leads us to an annexe across the street. We've paid for B and B, and she explains that we have to go back to the main building for our breakfast, shows us how to open and close the floor-to-ceiling window in our studio and how the air-conditioning works, and leaves. It's a large, smart and modern room, albeit with a number of drawers that don't open and shut properly, and will be fine for three or four days.

Georgioupoli itself is a mixture of old and new, a once-unspoilt undoubtedly pretty village at the mouth of the Almyros River that has sadly been overtaken by the presence of several large hotels, magnets it would appear for visitors from Eastern Europe. Taverna menus and A-boards are printed not only in the traditional Greek and English but in what we presume to be Russian. We're struck by the numbers of tourists wearing colour-coded wristbands, the badge of the all-inclusive hotel, and we wonder how many of them actually use the tavernas. What they probably don't realise is that at one euro sixty-five for a half-litre bottle, the Mythos lager in a local minimarket is almost twice what we paid yesterday in Chania and the most expensive Greek bottled beer we've seen on Crete.

But the gyros in one of the tavernas on the square are excellent and only two euros thirty a portion. Lunch with half a litre of white wine comes to less than ten euros.

Our pre-dinner drink, we decide, will be a glass of our Chania landlord Yiannis's own-brand red wine. Bad move.

When it's poured its colour is somewhere between a dark rosé wine and pale, weak tea and it tastes, well, it's hard to describe but it matches the colour. Not quite vinegar but something sharp and fairly undrinkable. Thankfully we have another bottle of wine with us, and that and the excellent house wine at the nearby Arolithos taverna quickly help us forget the taste of Yiannis's brew. The spetsofai (sausage stew) at Arolithos is excellent, even if the presentation is a little over-fussy, and at the end of the meal we get change out of thirty-euros. The all-inclusive visitors at the big hotels don't know what they're missing.

*

About two hundred metres off the Georgioupoli beach is the tiny islet of Agios Nikolaos, on which is perched a little whitewashed church of the same name. There's a narrow rocky causeway that leads to it and after breakfast and an hour relaxing on our generous balcony, we make our way across to it. It isn't easy going. The rocks under our feet make walking difficult, dangerous almost, as you feel that you could slip at any point and plunge into the sea. It's also a hot, sticky morning and the clouds have built up to the point where a few spots of rain begin to fall, making the rocks slippery and even more difficult to negotiate. But we make it.

There isn't a great deal to see when we get to Agios Nikolaos, but it's something you have to do if you're in Geogioupoli. The little church is, well, a little Greek church and that's all there is on the islet. But the view back towards the land is pretty spectacular. Straight ahead and just beyond the village the mountains of the Lefka Ori rise fairly dramatically. To the left is the long narrow sandy beach that stretches for ten kilometres, almost half the way to Rethymno, our next port of call. We take in the view, take a few photographs, then take the rocky causeway back to the village, thankfully under a now clear, cloudless sky.

According to our guidebook, Georgioupoli has been "swamped by coastal hotel development". That's a little unfair since a great deal of the village is still unspoilt, but there *are* three large and relatively new Corissa hotels right on the seafront. They're not necessarily all-inclusive because we occasionally see wrist-banded diners in the tavernas at lunchtime, but they do mean that there are normally plenty of tables available in the evening. A quick look on the company's website reveals that seven nights' half-board at this time of year costs fourteen hundred euros for two people in the cheapest room. That's a considerable amount more than a week doing it our way is costing.

At a large-ish grocery store called Anna Market we come across something we've rarely seen in a Greece shop before – red wine on draught. We're allowed to taste it first, and if we like it we can buy a refillable 75cl plastic bottleful of the stuff for two ninety-five. It's an offer we can't refuse. It's considerably better than the own-label plonk that Yiannis in Chania gave us.

A few doors down from Zorba's is Babis, a taverna that's been recommended to us by previous visitors. It's one of those places where they will always find you a table, no matter how busy they are, and they will never ask you to leave, even after you've finished your meal and there are people queuing at the door. Babis himself (we assume it's Babis) sits on a high stool at the back of the restaurant, cigarette permanently burning in an ashtray, his role being to look after the money. The wonderfully effervescent Mrs Babis supervises the service, keeping a motherly eye on the three young waiters, at least two of whom are her sons. We order a plate of fried courgettes as a shared starter, and they're delicious. But they're not enough, according to Mrs Babis.

"You need something else with that," she says when she inspects what we're eating, and returns a couple of minutes later with a dish of tzatziki "On the house." At the end of our meal, superb kleftiko, she brings us each a portion of brandy-soaked sponge cake and a glass of raki, also complimentary, and a bill for less than thirty euros. Probably the best dinner we've had since we left home.

CHAPTER NINE

Rethymno – "Buy your colanders inside"

The bus from Georgioupoli takes less than half an hour to reach Rethymno and costs six euros sixty each for a return ticket, and we're once again deposited at the bus station where we changed buses on our journey from Agia Galini to Chora Sfakion what seems like months ago. And it's only a couple of hundred metres' walk to the main reason why we've come here today, the massive Venetian fortress known simply as the Fortezza. But before we get there we visit the little church of Agios Spiridon, built into the cliff beneath the fortress and full of beautifully painted icons and swinging candleholders. We reach it by a staircase that gives us stunning views back across bay towards Georgioupoli and towards the Lefka Ori.

The Fortezza dominates Rethymno, and according to both written sources and more recent archaeological evidence was built on the site of the ancient acropolis of Rethimna. The foundation stone was laid in 1573 to combat raids on the city by pirates, but despite its imposing size it was unable to repel the Turks less than a century later. We pay our four euros admission fee and enjoy scrambling around the dusty low-level ruins, as well as visiting the restored Mosque of Sultan Ibrahim Han. When they conquered Rethymno in the seventeenth century, the Turks built their mosque on the site of the Catholic Cathedral of Agios Nikolaos (who else?). The architecture is spectacular, with a dome that is one of the largest in Greece supported by eight arches and a niche pointing in the direction of Mecca.

Outside, among the cooling pine trees, we find the Erofili Theatre, a small modern amphitheatre where we're treated to some charming entertainment by about a dozen pre-school-age children and their minders. It's a little like a rehearsal for a school nativity play – but the wrong season. They scream and screech with delight as their elders attempt to put some sort of order into their fun. We've no idea what's going on, of course, but what a joy it is to sit and watch.

*

It's very hot when we walk down into the old town but the narrow streets provide plenty of shade. The old quarter of Rethymno is a maze of lanes and alleys with tightly packed old houses, many of whose balconies are draped with flowers and plants. The Ottoman influence is everywhere in the mosques and minarets, and after being hassled and harried by the overly aggressive touts at the tavernas around the old Venetian harbour, we settle down on a breezy corner next to the Neratzes Mosque – converted from a church in the seventeenth century and now used as a concert venue – for a modestly priced lunch.

A few metres away, on Vernardou Street, we're treated to a free show by a practitioner of a dying art. The door to Yiorgos Hatziparaskos's bakery shop is open and an elderly woman who is almost certainly his wife Katerina stands in the doorway and beckons us to step inside. In the dim light, behind a large heavy wooden table, stands a man who's probably eighty, dressed in chef's whites and shorts and with a white pill-box hat on his head. This is Yiorgos himself, said to be one of the last traditional filo masters in Greece. Like an Italian pizza chef, he manipulates a ball of dough in his hands, slapping it down on the table from time to time. Then he whirls it into a giant bubble before stretching it over the table in a rough circle that's probably two metres in diameter. We watch in silence, awestruck. He looks up at us and smiles, then two younger assistants step forward and begin to prepare the wafer-thin pastry for baking. Katerina offers a tray and invites us to try some of the tastiest baklava we will probably ever experience. Never mind the Fortezza – this was worth the bus fare.

Further down the same street we're baffled by a printed notice in the window of a souvenir shop – "For another languets and colanders ask inside." Curious to find out why a souvenir shop should be selling kitchen utensils, why anyone would want to take an implement for washing and drying vegetables home as a memento of their Cretan holiday, we go inside. All is rapidly revealed. About half of the crowded little shop is taken up with displays of colourful calendars – views of Rethymno, views of Crete, views of Greece. Charming pictures of the ubiquitous Greek cats, saucy calendars showing the exposed backsides of young women, softly pornographic calendars based on Hellenic art. Barbara buys a beautiful lace tablecloth and we head back in the direction of the bus station.

Back in Georgioupoli we find what is generally reckoned to be the best restaurant in the village and one of the finest fish tavernas in the whole of Crete. Poseidon is tucked away down a narrow little lane and serves 'only fish', according to its A-board. It's owned by a fishing family, the seating area is all outside in a courtyard in the shade of mulberry trees and there's no printed menu. We're invited to choose from that day's catch laid out on a counter, then watch as it's cooked on a barbecue with the addition of a few herbs and served with a plate of chips. It's simple and delicious – and very popular with Germans.

CHAPTER TEN

Heraklion – Lounging on the Astroturf

It's rained, quite heavily at times, during the night and there's still a considerable amount of cloud around this morning. Cretan drains don't cope particularly well with rain, particularly downpours, and the dirt roads around Georgioupoli are dotted with large pools of water. I have a cup of coffee on the balcony, watch the owner of the clothing and souvenir shop across the street going through his morning ritual of wheeling racks of goods out onto the pavement, then go back inside and pack our bags for what is the penultimate time on Crete.

Our last significant journey on the island is the one-hundred-kilometre bus ride along the north coast to the capital Heraklion. It's only come from Chania, but the bus is already fifteen minutes late by the time it reaches us; however it's not terribly busy and we have no trouble finding seats together. It's an interesting journey, sometimes down at the water's edge, sometimes passing through little villages inland, and every now and again we have a light shower of rain. Two young people nearby annoy us a little by playing music on a smartphone, but by and large it's a comfortable enjoyable journey and by the time we reach Heraklion at about half past one it's a beautiful cloud-free day.

The hotel we've booked, the Kastro, is in the tongue-twisting Theotokopoulou Street, the best part of a kilometre from the bus station, and it takes us about twenty minutes of navigating the busy streets on foot to find it. It's modern, glass-fronted, clean and clinical and the staff are friendly. We're on the fifth floor and our room opens onto an Astroturfed roof garden with a couple of sun loungers, a sofa, an armchair and panoramic views over the city – quite different from anywhere we've stayed in Greece.

We have another new experience after we've unpacked a few things and gone out for a late lunch. We settle on a taverna on the old harbour and when we're seated a waiter brings us menus, along with a paper copy with our table number on it and a pen. We tick the boxes against the food and drink we want and hand it back to the waiter. It's different but it's popular because even at two-thirty on a Wednesday afternoon it's very busy.

Enjoying an alfresco dinner in the Plateia Venizelou, a few hundred metres down from the hotel, we get into conversation with our waiter, a young man who's eager to talk. After the usual formalities of asking us where we're from and what we're doing and how long we've been on Crete he tells us how well he knows and how much he loves England.

"My sister works in London," he says. "She is a doctor at Great Ormond Street Hospital. I am training to be a doctor also." We're naturally impressed. "But I don't like London," he goes on. "It's too big and noisy for me. I like Newcastle – I have friends there, I have been many times. But I can't understand what people are saying." We smile and tell him not to worry, we can't understand them either.

Lounging on the roof of the Kastro at eleven on a beautiful starlit evening, sipping a large Metaxa, gazing absent-mindedly over the Heraklion rooftops and musing on the thought that we have only one more full day on Crete, I suddenly become aware of a gradually increasing sound, a rising torrent of noise heading towards me. And then it rears up from behind the houses, a passenger jet leaving Nikos Kazantzakis International Airport five kilometres away and heading into the western sky. It goes directly over the hotel and it's so close as it passes over my head I feel I can almost touch it.

*

There's a feeling, a hope almost, as we take the early bus out to Knossos that we may have saved the best for last. Only five kilometres south of Heraklion, this is the jewel in Crete's crown, the capital of the Minoan civilisation. We've been advised by the receptionist at the Kastro to get there early to avoid the crowds and the heat, but even at nine in the morning there are probably a dozen coaches in the car park already and a similar number of parties being ushered around by their guides. Our ten-euro entrance fee also includes admission to the Heraklion Archaeological Museum, which we plan to visit this afternoon, so for such an important site we reckon that's good value.

It's impossible not to be impressed. Often called 'Europe's oldest city' and said to be home to a hundred thousand people in its heyday, the first palace at Knossos was built around 1900 BC, destroyed by an earthquake and rebuilt in a much grander style. It was partially destroyed again sometime between 1500 and 1450 BC, but the Minoans continued to live there until the palace was finally burned down. The ruins were first uncovered by Cretan archaeologists in the 1870s, and in 1894 the English journalist and adventurer Arthur Evans came here. He spent thirty-five years and, it's estimated, £250,000 of his own money, excavating and, more controversially, reconstructing parts of the site. We come away from Knossos with the impression that it was more about what Evans thought it had looked like and been used for rather than the way it had actually been.

He looked at the ruins that he'd excavated and, in many cases put two and two together in an attempt to reconstruct a 3,500-year-old palace. We can't help wondering if he didn't come up with five at times. And we're not the only ones, apparently. We read later that many archaeologists also believe that Evans sacrificed accuracy to his own fantasy. But Knossos is still an awesome 'must see' place, even if so many areas have had to be roped off to prevent them from further damage caused by the 120,000 pairs of feet that stamp around the site each year.

We take the bus back into Heraklion for a late lunch at a taverna opposite the Archaeological Museum, then visit the museum itself. Like Knossos, it's heaving with guided tours, many of the coach parties clearly on the same itinerary as our own. As a result, it's noisy and uncomfortable but it has its benefits since we're able to learn more about the exhibits by eavesdropping on the commentaries of the English-speaking guides. The museum is packed with treasures – pottery, jewellery, sarcophagi – from the Minoan settlements on the island, including the 3,600-year-old Phaestos Disk, one of the many artefacts that have been moved to here from one of the first sites we visited on Crete.

About the size of a CD, the disk was discovered in 1908 and is etched with more than two hundred and forty early Minoan pictographic images in a continuous spiral. It repeats itself several times as it coils in from the edge to the centre, leading some experts to believe that it may be a prayer, but in truth it has never been deciphered. It's a magical, mystical object – and in its own way it's a powerful symbol of all we have loved about Crete.

Barbara waiting at the quayside for another ferry

On the road again – about to board a bus on the Peloponnese

Indulging in one of my favourite Greek pastimes

Our friendly bus driver on Folegandros

Arriving on another island – the little harbour of Iraklia

Tempting sign at an Amorgos taverna

Irapetra, Crete – Napoleon
was here, possibly

Chania, Crete, at sunset

Monemvasia – Greece's Gibraltar

*Neapoli – what kind of
place have we come to?*

*Aeropoli – birthplace
of a revolution*

The world's biggest turkey

Symi – 'the most beautiful harbour in Greece'

Kalymnos – patriotic hillside decoration

A collector's item – the municipal bus on Kalymnos

The picturesque harbour at Katsadia, Lipsi

No entry – on the door of the cathedral in Kos

Selfie at the end of our travels

PART THREE

The Peloponnese

CHAPTER ONE

Corinth – "If I speak in the tongues of men..."

The little suburban train rattles westward along the Saronic Gulf coast towards Isthmia, the town that gave the English language the word for a narrow strip of land between two stretches of water, at the mouth of the Corinth Canal. To our left the shoreline isn't the most attractive we've seen in Greece, lined as it is with the warehouses, shipyards and dockyards that remind visitors of Greek's past as a great seafaring nation. To the right, faded green hills rise steeply, populated with little farms and herds of goats.

When I was a child growing up in the 1950s my parents had an ancient illustrated encyclopaedia, two of whose photographs held a particular fascination for me, black and white pictures of places I determined to visit when I grew up. I never knew why those two in particular, but one picture was of the Needles, the three chalk stacks off the western tip of the Isle of Wight, the other of a ship squeezing its way through the Corinth Canal. It was about fifteen years ago when I finally got to the place known simply in the South of England as 'the Island', and while I was excited at finally seeing the Needles, I was a little disappointed. They were nowhere near as tall as I'd imagined, erosion no doubt having taken its toll in the decades since I'd stared at that photograph. The canal, on the other hand, which I finally saw a couple of years later, lived up to all expectations.

On our first visit to the Peloponnese we took an organised excursion from our base in Tolon that included a visit to the ancient site at Epidavros and a trip through the Corinth Canal. It was a beautiful June day as our little tourist boat cruised through the canal and back again, a return journey of no more than thirteen kilometres that lasted less than an hour and a half but it was a magical, almost spiritual, experience nonetheless. The Roman emperor Nero began building the canal in the first century AD but the project wasn't completed until 1893. The sheer walls of the trench towered a hundred metres above us in places and, even though the canal's twenty metres wide at its narrowest, there were times when you felt you could stretch out and reach both sides at the same time. Today, our train crosses from the Greek mainland to the Peloponnese peninsula fifty metres above the canal. We get the briefest glimpse of the water beneath us but it's enough to send a shiver down my spine and remind me again of that black-and-white photograph.

We'd assumed, read somewhere perhaps, that the train would take us into the modern town of Corinth and that we'd be able to get a bus or a taxi the eight kilometres to Ancient Corinth, where we've booked accommodation for a couple of nights. When we leave the train we expect to find ourselves in the centre of a busy little town, but what is clearly Corinth Station is surrounded by – nothing. All around are fields and open space and there isn't a house, or any other sort of building, in sight. Just outside the station building, however, there is a bus stop. We make our way over to it but nowhere is there a timetable, nor any sign that it's been used recently.

"No bus," says the only other person to have left the train here, a Greek woman in her early twenties. We look at her with expressions that say, "So what the hell are we supposed to do now?"

"You wait here for taxi," she says in answer to our silent question.

And so we do, for about ten minutes until a single black Mercedes saloon arrives, as if from nowhere. The driver, a tall man of about forty, jumps out and begins a conversation with the young woman. Then, without warning, he turns to us, lifts our bags into the boot of the Merc and gestures us to get in the back seat. We show him a piece of paper on which is written the address of our accommodation in Old Corinth and he nods and mumbles, "OK," then turns to the young woman and says something that we assume to be "I'll be back in fifteen minutes" or similar, climbs into the driving seat and pulls away with an almighty screeching of tyres.

Throughout the ten-minute journey the driver keeps up a conversation on his smartphone, skilfully manoeuvring the car along a narrow twisting road with one hand until he stops outside Vasilios Marinos Rooms. He deposits our bags on the terrace, accepts the ten-euro note we offer and drives off, tyres screeching again.

There's a door on one side of the building that we assume leads to the accommodation and an empty taverna on the other, but no one appears to be around. We walk nervously towards the taverna and call "Hello" in that quiet, almost whispered way you do when you don't really want to disturb anyone. Eventually a small attractive woman of about fifty who we assume to be Mrs Marinos appears from the kitchen, smiles, shakes our hands and wishes us "Welcome." She leads us to the closed door at the other side of the building where, despite being no more than five feet tall and probably weighing less than both of us, she picks up both of our bags and bounds up a flight of stairs to the first-floor landing. We're out of breath just trying to keep up with her.

She opens the door to our room, gives us the key and tells us we can get breakfast downstairs any time after eight in the morning, then disappears again. The Marinos family has apparently been renting rooms in Corinth for more than fifty years and the studio is spacious and comfortable, although it's at the back of the building and the view over an untidy yard leaves something to be desired. There's more than adequate compensation, however, as I sit on the balcony with a cup of tea and spot two birds scuttling around the base of the garden's only tree. They're about the size of a small pigeon, sandy-coloured, with a long, pointed beak and a distinctive black and white crown of feathers on their heads. I have no idea what they might be, but ornithologically-aware Barbara recognises them immediately.

"Hoopoes," she says with the air of someone who sees them every day. Google tells me she's right and suggests we're quite lucky.

*

Corinth has been devastated by earthquakes so many times in its history and was completely destroyed in 1858 when the new town was built eight kilometres to the north – or quite close to where the train dropped us off earlier. The few modern homes, tavernas and gift shops around the historic site that make up the present-day village of Ancient Corinth exist merely to serve the needs of tourists and travellers. Many of those who come here are on day trips from Athens, as evidenced by the lines of coaches outside the historic site this afternoon. But by the evening they've gone and there's only ourselves and a handful of other visitors to share our custom among the tavernas.

It's a balmy twenty-four degrees Celsius when we walk the couple of hundred metres into the village for dinner. We choose Marinos, so keeping it in the family presumably, and sit on their large open terrace, watching the sun set over the Gulf of Corinth and enjoying an excellent meal and a half-litre of house red wine that costs three euros. Apart from a table of six priests, we're the only customers. The bill when it comes is just scribbled on a piece of paper, no printed details, no VAT number as required by law. There is a suggestion that Greece is about to default on the latest instalment of the repayment of its international debt. It makes you think.

*

We're woken around seven on a warm but disappointingly overcast morning by a cacophony of sounds – birds, insects, goats in a field just behind our building. Breakfast downstairs is served by the woman who greeted us yesterday and a man we assume is Mr Marinos and is a real feast – orange juice, spinach pie, omelette with vegetables, yogurt with quince (so Mr Marinos tells us) and melon and apricots, with as much tea or coffee as we can drink. It's all included in the cost of our room and when we've finished we're not sure whether we'll need to eat for the remainder of the day.

When we're thoroughly sated we ask Mr Marinos about the best way to reach our next planned destination, Nafplion. We know we can get a bus there from Isthmia but we're not sure how to get from here to the bus station. We assume there's a bus service from the village into modern Corinth and a connection there.

Mr Marinos thinks for a moment. "You *could* get a bus," he says. "But there's no timetable and sometimes they don't come all day. The best way to the bus station in Isthmia is probably by taxi."

We've seen the village's cabs, two or three of them, outside the entrance to the archaeological site. "How much would that cost?" I ask.

Mr Marinos shrugs his shoulders. "Fifteen euros, maybe twenty. I can arrange it for you. What time do you want to go?"

We've looked at bus timetables and are sure we can pick up the service that runs from Athens to Nafplion in Isthmia at around midday. "Eleven o'clock," I say.

"Okay," he says with a smile. "My cousin will be here at eleven."

It stays dull for the remainder of the day. There are short, sporadic periods of sunshine but it's predominantly grey and heavy. There are already about a dozen coaches outside when we walk over to the ancient site and pay our six-euro admission fees, and as soon as we're inside the fence the fact that the weather is somewhat less than perfect no longer seems to matter. It's a wonderful experience, the site itself being dominated by the seven remaining pillars of the Temple of Apollo, built around 550 BC and one of the oldest remaining temples in Greece. Despite the presence of so many coaches, there don't seem to be that many visitors, certainly only a handful of groups faithfully following a guide holding aloft an unopened umbrella, and as we walk among the largely Roman ruins we are moved when we remember that we're walking in the footsteps of St Paul. Just outside the site, in fact, is a large stone plinth on which the words of Paul's First Epistle to the Corinthians are etched in Greek and English. "If I speak in the tongues of men and angels, but have not love, I am a noisy gong or a clanging cymbal," and so on.

We're also following a path that was trodden by Pausanias, the man who inadvertently invented travel writing and the guidebook. He was actually a Roman who came here in the second century AD and his account of his travels in the Peloponnese is pretty much the first guidebook that exists anywhere. It seems that he wasn't very widely read by his contemporaries, but his work was rediscovered by travellers in the early nineteenth century and was reprinted in English as recently as 2006.

The museum on the site houses an impressive collection of statues, mosaics and friezes and in one room tells the story of an audacious theft in 1990. A hoard of priceless ancient artefacts, many of which had been unearthed in Corinth by the American School of Classical Studies since 1896 and included the rare marble head of a statue dating from 470 BC, was stolen from the museum one night, along with a million drachmas (about three thousand US dollars) in cash, the wages of the site's staff. They had apparently been stolen to order by a notorious local gang and found their way across the Atlantic. Acting on a tip-off, police found almost all of the two hundred and eighty antiquities wrapped in plastic and hidden in fish crates in a storage area in Miami nine years later. One Greek man was found guilty of the original theft and sentenced to life imprisonment; two others were acquitted. An intriguing story that adds to the enjoyment of our visit.

Chapter Two

Nafplion – 857 steps... or is it 999?

We've enjoyed another massive breakfast served by the ever-smiling Mr and Mrs Marinos and are packed and downstairs by just before eleven. It's been raining on and off all night and the forecast for today is for more rain to come, although hopefully it will have cleared by the time we reach Nafplion, sixty kilometres south as the crow flies and a settlement we've seen described as the "prettiest large town in the Peloponnese." Back in the day it was an important port and it was the first capital of independent Greece from 1827 to 1834, when Athens took over, and we've no doubt that there'll be no shortage of interesting and historical quarters to keep us occupied. It will also be a useful hub for visiting a couple of other places on our Peloponnese to-do list.

Mr Marinos's cousin arrives on the stroke of eleven and as we thank and say goodbye to our hosts, he loads our bags into the boot of the inevitable Mercedes. The journey to the smart modern bus station outside Isthmia takes about twenty minutes through some fairly flat and uninteresting countryside and leaves us with more than half an hour to wait for our bus. I offer the taxi driver a twenty-euro note and he starts to find change. I tell him not to bother, and he smiles and drives off. Our tickets cost seven euros fifty each for the ninety-minute journey and the bus is packed. We spend most of the time sitting apart and it's only when at least half of our fellow passengers disembark at Argos – the town, that is, not the store – that we're able to spend the last half-hour and dozen or so kilometres together.

We reach the centre of Nafplion, according to some people the most elegant town on the Greek mainland, at around one-thirty. The bus station is on Syngrou, and Eudokia, the studio complex where we've booked accommodation, is no more than a hundred metres along the same street. The front door is open so we let ourselves in and take the little lift to the first floor. There's no one around and our calls of "Hello – is there anyone there?" seem to fall on deaf ears. It's only after I use the bathroom in one of the apartments whose front door has been left open that an elderly woman appears from the floor above, alerted, no doubt, by the sound of the toilet being flushed.

She doesn't speak much English, but a combination of Barbara's Greek and sight of some of our documents convinces her that we're bona fide guests and not potential squatters. But we're too early, she manages to explain to us. Our room won't be ready for at least another hour, but if we want, we can leave our bags with her and come back later. It's still dull and spitting with rain from time to time, but having taken up her offer we sit under the awning of a café on Syntagma Square in the heart of the first capital of independent Greece, enjoy a drink and watch dozens of children as they make their way home from school, each trying to outshine their classmates with their newly acquired fidget-spinner skills.

Back at Eudokia an hour or so later, the elderly woman, who we've somehow discovered is the owner Eudokia's mother, lets us into our smart, well-furnished room and goes through a lengthy comic routine showing us how the wi-fi works. A password on a piece of paper would have been enough.

The cafés and tavernas on Bouboulinas, the broad street that looks out towards the little island fortress of Bourtzi, half a kilometre offshore, are quiet, almost deserted this evening, but the narrow streets in the old town are busy. The temperature has dipped into an unseasonal mid-teens and while a few hardy souls are eating outside most diners are packed into the tavernas. But this being Greece, however busy they are they will still find a place for two more. In the end we plump for Aiolos, which we read later in our guidebook is a "homely taverna" with "some excellent food". We can't disagree with that. What the book doesn't mention are the added extras – the dips for starters, the sponge cake with slices of apple in cinnamon and the little jug of raki. And a bill for less than thirty euros. We love Nafplion already.

*

Another dull, grey morning with a temperature that's forecast to reach no higher than twenty. But that's something of a blessing, since this morning we plan to visit the Palamidi Castle, the massive Venetian fortress that was built early in the eighteenth century and towers some two hundred metres above the town. There are two ways to reach the summit. The easier option is a taxi, but at the rank by the bus station the return fare is advertised at twenty euros, including twenty minutes' waiting time. Since twenty minutes doesn't seem long enough to do the place justice, and twenty euros seems too much for a journey that will probably take no more than ten minutes each way, we go for the alternative, more traditional way, walking.

We've been warned that it's a steep climb and it won't be easy. The number of steps we have to tackle varies, depending on who you ask about them or which guidebook you read, from eight hundred and fifty-seven, which sounds like an accurate figure, to nine hundred and ninety-nine, a little dubious and too rounded, to 'thousands', the taxi drivers' version, presumably. Whichever is correct, it's still a daunting task and best tackled on a day like this. It's cool and breezy, a boon since there's very little shade on the way up. We take frequent stops to admire the view and gather our breath, and when we reach the summit after about forty-five minutes we discover that it's National Museums Day and the usual four-euro admission charge has been waived.

It's well worth the effort. There are some wonderful views over the town and the surrounding countryside, although these would undoubtedly be even better were it not for the low cloud, and large numbers of ruined buildings, most of them built by the Venetians in the early years of the eighteenth century. The paths that guide us through the site are well laid out and signposted, full of surprises and hidden nooks and crannies. We spend some time marvelling at the wonder of it all and being buffeted by the wind, then make our way back down into the town. Going back down takes less than twenty minutes, and we reward ourselves for our efforts with a beer at a pavement café and a discussion about what to do next.

Since it's National Museums Day and they're all free we feel somewhat spoiled for choice. The Archaeological Museum on Syntagma Square has not long since reopened after a lengthy closure for restoration. It's housed in a Venetian arsenal, itself a beautiful and historically important building in its own right, and is home to what is said to be one of the finest collections in the Peloponnese – pottery, suits of armour, artefacts from the Mycean period – all conveniently displaying explanations in Greek and English. We would have been more than happy to pay three euros for the privilege.

This evening we go to Vassilis, a taverna that our guidebook says is "one of the better bets" and a "popular family-run place". The visit starts well. It's relatively quiet when we arrive and we get some very attentive initial service. Sadly, within fifteen minutes a thirty- or forty-strong party of what we assume are students arrives. Some, but not all, are American and very loud and the overall noise level makes it impossible to have a normal conversation. One pair of diners actually asks to be moved outside into the street, despite the less than summery weather and the absence of patio heaters. The food is good, particularly the recommended rabbit stifado, but the waiters have obviously been told to concentrate on the students and the service suffers as a result.

But there's good news on the horizon. Although the green signs outside the pharmacies are still showing temperatures in the high teens when we walk back to Eudokia, the wind has dropped and the forecast is for warm and dry weather and an end to the clouds and rain that have dogged our Peloponnese experience so far.

*

When we first came to this part of Greece together in the mid-noughties much of the holiday accommodation was operated by a single British tour company. That was before the financial crisis of 2008, when the company went belly-up after the Icelandic bank that was the major shareholder in its parent company crashed. Having booked a holiday on one of the islands with them, we were among the victims, but we managed to extricate ourselves, rebook with someone else and get our money back fairly quickly. For other people it took over a year before they were reimbursed. But today we're keen to see how Tolon, the little seaside town where we had stayed, has fared this last decade and to revisit the nearby ancient site of Asini.

For the first time in almost a week it's a beautiful sunny morning without a cloud in the sky and we're able to enjoy the luxury of having breakfast on our little balcony. There are one or two minor twinges in the legs as a result of our climb up to the Palamidi Castle yesterday, but they *are* only minor and we're more than ready for the day ahead. The buses to Tolon leave every hour and the twenty-minute journey costs us one euro twenty cents each. We're dropped just outside the town and walk the short distance back to Asini.

The city that once existed on this site was mentioned by Homer in the *Iliad* and is said to have been founded almost five thousand years ago. Our friend Pausanias even visited and wrote about the site in the second century. But there followed centuries of neglect and it wasn't until the 1920s that Swedish archaeologists excavated the ruins and put Asini back on Greece's historical map. Like many occupiers who had gone before them, however, Italian troops during the Second World War appreciated its elevated position overlooking the bay that leads into the harbour at Nafplion and established their machine gun nests here. Nor were they too fussy about how they treated the site, and much of what had survived the centuries was vandalised. Sixty years on, when we made our first visit, it was neglected and overgrown, a few unidentified piles of stones, and we weren't even sure we were in the right place.

But since then it appears that almost a million euros has been poured in, much, it goes without saying, from the EU, creating safe paved walkways, information boards and small exhibition halls. There's no doubt that we're in the right place this time. And I'd forgotten how beautiful was the view, across the little bay to Tolon itself.

It's clear that Tolon has struggled since the financial crash. It is very pretty and benefits from having what were once regarded as the best beaches on the Peloponnese, but today has a downmarket feel to it and there appear to be as many tavernas and accommodation blocks that are either boarded up or displaying 'For Sale' signs as there are establishments that are actually operating. Nevertheless, we find the ever-so-slightly bizarrely named Gorillas taverna on the beach, chill out and enjoy some excellent food.

*

In contrast to Asini, Mycenae has had hundreds of millions pumped into it over the years and is rightly regarded as one of the jewels in the Peloponnese crown, if not the whole of Greece. Indeed, the Lion Gate through which you enter the site is believed to be the oldest monumental structure in Europe, and there are historians and archaeologists who regard Mycenae as the most important and awesome ancient site on the continent. We're up at a reasonable time on a second successive bright sunny morning to see for ourselves.

The ten o'clock bus from Nafplion has a short stop in Argos and arrives at Mycenae at around eleven and costs us four euros each. It's still quiet with only a couple of coaches in the car park, although this is almost certainly a lull between two storms. We pay our eight-euro entry fee and spend a leisurely couple of hours exploring this amazing place. There has been a settlement on this site since the sixth millennium BC and it was the headquarters of King Agamemnon, the brother-in-law of Helen of Troy. For centuries it was one of Greece's best-kept secrets. The locals were always aware of its existence but no one else took much interest until the German amateur archaeologist Heinrich Schliemann started excavating the site in the 1870s. Since then it's been recognised as having been the power base of one of the region's most important kingdoms for more than four hundred years and a major influence over much of the rest of Greece.

The tourists who arrive in their coachloads seem to stay for not much more than an hour, swarming over the ruins like armies of ants, then whizzing through the museum and heading back to their coaches. They've presumably got to 'do' Ancient Corinth this afternoon so have no time to dally. We have the luxury of choosing which bus we will take back to Nafplion, so we take things at a somewhat more sedate pace, leaving ourselves time to grab a slice of pizza and a can of beer from a mobile catering unit in the car park before returning.

Chapter Three

Sparta – "Just mention my name..."

It's another warm bright morning and we're up early. After breakfast in our room, we say goodbye to Eudokia's mother and wheel our bags the one hundred metres up the road to the bus station and buy two tickets for the eight-thirty bus to Tripoli. Seventy kilometres south of Nafplion, Tripoli is the capital of the Peloponnese and the administrative centre of the Arcadia region, not a place to linger long, according to the guidebook. But being in the centre it's an important transport hub, and as such, it's where we'll change buses to reach our ultimate destination for today, Sparta.

The crowded bus heads north-west and negotiates the busy narrow streets of Argos – the founder of the store chain was, apparently, on holiday in the area when he first had the idea for his shops – then turns and heads south-west, across a fertile plain green with vineyards, olive groves and orchards of oranges and lemons. We climb into higher, less productive country, through a dramatic mountain landscape on to a smart new highway that passes through several tunnels until it descends into a valley and reaches the new bus station in an untidy area on the outskirts of Tripoli an hour and a half later. We have time to enjoy a late breakfast of a pastry and a coffee before our connecting service to Sparta is ready to leave.

This time the less busy bus avoids the modern motorway and follows an older road due south through the mountains, snow-capped peaks rising to our left and right, until we pull into the bus station at Sparta. We know that our hotel, the Dioscouri, is on Lycourgou Street, and as we leave the bus station we realise that we are already on Lycourgou Street. As long as we take the right direction, we should have no trouble walking there. What we don't realise is that the street dissects the town centre, is more than a kilometre long and slopes steadily up from the bus station at the bottom to the Dioscouri near the top. The pavements are uneven, there are numerous side streets to cross and, as a result, it takes us more than half an hour of hard luggage hauling to reach the hotel.

Tired and sweaty, we drag our bags up the steps at the front of the hotel into a smart reception area and are greeted by a young man in his twenties who introduces himself as Dimitri.

"You like good Greek food?" he asks us after the formalities of checking in have been completed. Of course we do. Dimitri hands us a business card for a taverna called Diethnes.

"It's just a short walk from here," he says. "My friend Takis runs it. If you go there, be sure to mention my name. He will look after you."

With the prospect of some special Greek hospitality ahead, we take the lift to our fourth-floor room, briefly enjoy the spectacular views over the city from our balcony and set off to explore the ruins of the historic ancient city. And there *are* plenty of ruins – but not all of them marked. Sparta is a modern city built largely on top of an ancient one. Local laws dictate that when a developer unearths a slice of the old city his planned new building has to stop. The site is then roped off and left untouched until the funds are available for a proper excavation to take place. In the current economic climate that could be decades hence, and in the meantime central Sparta is dotted with little roped-off plots of what look like derelict land.

*

At the top of modern Sparta's other main street, Konstantinou Palaiologou, in front of a sports stadium, stands an impressive statue of Leonidas, immortalised in the 2006 Hollywood film *300*. According to Herodotus, Leonidas led three hundred brave Greek warriors in a stand against over five million Persians at Thermopylae, although later historians have put the numbers at more like a thousand against a hundred and fifty thousand. It was, nevertheless, a remarkable feat, holding back the Persian advance long enough for the Greeks to regroup. Sadly, there isn't much more of Sparta that's worth visiting today. The ruins of the ancient Acropolis are scattered and, while not entirely neglected, overgrown and confusing, and we don't spend too much time scrambling over them. But once you reach the theatre at the top of the site, once one of the biggest auditoria in Greece, the views across to the Taygetos Mountains are breathtaking. Especially when, as now, some of their peaks are still snow-capped.

Tucked away in a side street off Konstantinou Palaiologou is a little taverna where we sit outside and enjoy a late lunch of excellent gyros and a half-litre of white wine for the princely sum of seven euros fifty – that's for both of us – before we return to the hotel. Bizarrely, someone has changed the television in our room while we've been out. We now have a modern flat-screen set instead of the old box that was there before, but we still can't find any English-language channels on it. But the room does have a strong wi-fi signal. Our eldest daughter is getting married shortly after we get back home, I need a new suit and Barbara has had an email to say that Marks and Spencer have a twenty-per-cent-off sale for the next couple of days. I spend the next half-hour browsing their website until I find what looks like something that appears appropriate for the father of the bride at a fairly informal register office wedding, and which I can subsequently wear on the odd occasions when a suit is called for. I click on the 'Buy now' button, then text my next-door neighbour Dan and ask him to look out for the parcel. The wonders of modern technology!

It's relatively quiet and tranquil at this end of Sparta before, at about six-thirty, the peace is shattered by the strange, but somewhat tuneful, peal of the bells of a large church across the street, the Evangelistria Cathedral. Something to look forward to tomorrow morning!

On Dimitri's advice we seek out the Diethnes taverna. In truth, it isn't difficult to find, since we've walked past it already on our way to the ancient Acropolis. We're greeted cordially by a tall man of about forty who answers with a curt "Yes" when we ask if he's Takis.

"We're staying at the Dioscouri," I tell him. "Dimitri said we should come here." That should be good for a free dessert or half a litre of house wine, I reckon. But Takis is unimpressed. In between serving us he sits at a pavement table outside, smoking and talking to two other men. It's a good meal, and at twenty-four euros we can't complain about the price, but we leave a little disappointed that the hospitality hasn't been a little warmer.

*

Just outside the hotel is a bus stop from where the service to Mystras departs. Built in the thirteenth century on a spur of Mount Taygetos, this was once an imposing town where the

Byzantine world seems to live on, and we've been told that visiting it is an absolute must. It's only five kilometres from Sparta, but in the short time that it takes the bus to weave its way out of the city into the hills the weather changes dramatically. The sky darkens until it feels more like midnight than midday and as we step off the bus heavy rain begins to fall. We pay our five-euro admission fee and are offered the opportunity by the guide, Ilias, a short Greek man of about fifty with shoulder-length dark hair and quirky but totally fluent English, the option of a shorter tour to avoid getting wet.

Barbara has taken the precaution of bringing her small umbrella and is naturally keen on the full two-and-a-half hour walk from the top of the extensive site to the bottom. I have to go along with it. It rains for at least half of the time we're there and I do get very wet. But the rain does eventually stop, even if the low cloud never entirely clears to reveal a proper view of the magnificent scenery, but it's all well worth it.

Mystras is as awesome as the guidebooks have us believe. It's a huge site that's only properly appreciated once you've walked through it and are down below looking up again. It thrived over five centuries under various regimes, but by the time of Greece's independence in 1822 it had been virtually abandoned and was in ruins. Restoration has been going on since the 1950s and it is now a Unesco World Heritage Site. And it's still the home of a convent occupied by a group of serene nuns making a living selling beautifully embroidered items. We've already been stunned by Ancient Corinth and Mycenae on this leg of our travels. In its own way Mystras is possibly more impressive.

A late lunch of moussaka and giouvetsi in a taverna in the new village of Mystras, in the shelter of the old city, enables me to dry out before we take the bus back into Sparta.

CHAPTER FOUR

Monemvasia – "Someone will have to pay"

There's an almost eerie silence in the dining room of the Dioscouri where we enjoy the five-euro all-you-can-eat buffet breakfast before returning to our room and getting our bags ready for the next bus journey. We can't believe how quiet it is – until the peace is shattered by a marching band heading towards the hotel from lower down Lycourgou Street. The band is followed by a disorderly troop of young soldiers, out of step but carrying rifles, which I suppose gives them a certain licence to march as they please. They settle down outside the main door of the Evangelistria across the street, and the band strikes up the National Anthem as people begin leaving the church. It's an odd sight, since everyone leaving the church is holding what appears to be a small bowl of muesli and a white plastic spoon. It's the feast of St Constantine, the first Orthodox emperor, and his mother Ayia Eleni, apparently. But why the muesli? There's no one around who speaks enough English for us to ask.

It takes us about half as long to walk back down to the bus station as it took us to reach our hotel a couple of days ago. For which we're thankful, since it's a warm morning and all trace of the rain that blighted our visit to Mystras has disappeared. We buy our single tickets for Monemvasia, the so-called 'Gibraltar of Greece', grab a couple of sandwiches and a Diet Coke from the bus station café and board an old and rather shabby bus that will take us the one hundred kilometres across Laconia to the little village of Gefyra, separated from Monemvasia by a narrow causeway.

We rattle through some rather uninspiring countryside, the road depressingly lined with rusting, derelict factories and the occasional military base, and through a series of small nondescript towns and villages until after about two and a half hours we reach Gefyra. There are only three other people left on the bus by this time, two of whom are a young couple who have asked the driver to drop them opposite a small modern supermarket. As they're leaving the bus we suddenly realise that immediately to our right is a sign announcing "Mpalkoni," which is pronounced 'balcony' (Barbara is constantly reminding me that 'mp' in Greek is pronounced 'b') and is where we've booked to stay for the next three nights. I rush down to the front of the bus.

"We'd like to get off here," I tell the driver, a short, smiling man of about fifty.

"But this isn't the bus stop," he says, pointing out the narrow road ahead. "We have to go down there."

"But we're staying here," I say. "Just here on the right. Balcony."

The driver's smile grows even wider, as if Mpalkoni is owned by his brother, and he switches off the bus's engine and climbs down onto the pavement, followed by Barbara and me. He removes our bags from the luggage hold, shakes my hand and wishes us a happy stay in Gefyra, then climbs back into the bus to complete what remains of his journey. The entrance to

Mpalkoni is a flight of stairs to the right of a small, dimly lit minimarket and we haul our bags up to reception to be greeted by our landlord Giorgios. The room we've booked is smallish with a bed that takes up almost all of the space that isn't occupied by the kitchenette and the bathroom. But it's well stocked with tea, coffee, milk and all sorts of other goodies and has a wonderful view – our first – of the magical rock that is Monemvasia. The downside appears to be rather patchy wi-fi.

And there's more to Gefyra than a stopping-off point for the Rock, we discover when we go out later for dinner. It's a genuine little Greek fishing village, with a collection of waterside tavernas with views across the harbour. We seek out Scorpios, whose business cards are in our reception area, and enjoy an excellent meal watching the fishing boats coming and going. With change out of thirty euros.

*

The sun is streaming into our studio at seven in the morning, but despite the fact that we're above a shop on the main road in and out of the village it's remarkably quiet. But very windy. As we sit on our little balcony and enjoy the view, the full, dramatic beauty of Monemvasia gradually takes us over. The left-wing writer Yiannis Ritsos, one of Greece's greatest poets, was born here in 1909 and his bust stands outside the house where he grew up. He wrote about the locality, "This scenery is as harsh as silence". We're not sure what he meant, but it is certainly breath-taking, and after breakfast we set out to walk across the narrow, man-made causeway to try and find out. The causeway was built in the sixth century, two hundred years after Monemvasia has been severed from the mainland by an earthquake. It takes about half an hour to reach the gateway to the Rock, a half-hour that's largely spent trying not to step into the path of the cars and small coaches that drive all the way up to the door. They can't get in, of course, it's too narrow, and they have to perform multiple-point turns and go back to where they started.

Rising up out of the sea in a manner that does indeed invite comparisons with Gibraltar, Monemvasia was a Byzantine stronghold, first settled in the sixth century but, unlike Mystras, it was never abandoned and people have continued to live here. It's all little cobbled lanes, trendy boutiques selling art and jewellery, upscale hotels and not-so-cheap bars and tavernas. Fortunately, the locals and the incomers who bought homes and businesses here have had the sense to conserve its beauty, meaning that development on the Rock has been carefully controlled. It has gained a name as something of an artists' colony, and, as long as nothing bigger than a handcart can get through its gateway, its future should be assured.

We visit the thirteenth-century cathedral, which is no bigger than a small English parish church, and, on the opposite side of the little square, the town museum, have a coffee outside one of the cafés on the main alley, and then, because there's no ATM on the Rock and we're running short of cash, decide to go back across the causeway and return to Monemvasia tomorrow. We have a wonderful relaxed lunch in the less busy Charamis on the harbour – pita gyros, salad, half a litre of white wine, twelve euros – buy some postcards and return to Mpalkoni to while away the rest of the afternoon.

This afternoon I finished reading *Mani*, Patrick Leigh Fermor's account of his travels in the southern Peloponnese in the 1950s, one of the inspirations for this leg of our travels. His idiosyncratic style can be hard work at times, but his love of Greece and the Greeks, his erudition and his knowledge of the history, religion and mythology make the effort very worthwhile. This has been a very appropriate place to read *Mani* and, unknown to us now, in a week or two's time we will visit the taverna where Leigh Fermor allegedly stayed when he was writing it.

We're down at the waterside this evening, dining at Votsala, a little taverna with a limited menu where an elderly woman who appears to be both owner and chef explains what's on offer. We're the last people in and the last out, so quiet is it this evening, but as ever on these occasions we're under no pressure to leave. So we sit and enjoy a second half-litre of house red and discuss how we're going to get to what we have decided will be our next destination.

*

Gefyra has a special charm, a uniquely Greek quality about it that would exist even without the amazing Monemvasia across the causeway. It is like many villages that hover somewhere between old fishing community and new tourist resort, but, sad to say, it probably wouldn't flourish without Monemvasia. It's too far from a decent airport, the ferries no longer call here and the roads in and out leave a great deal to be desired. Sad to say, it wouldn't attract very many visitors on its own merits.

The stiff breeze that blew for most of yesterday has largely died down, the sun's beating down from a cloudless sky and it's as warm as we've experienced since we've been on the Peloponnese. Nevertheless, after breakfast we head across the causeway again to get a second helping of the Rock. When we were there yesterday, we were taken by a poster we'd seen in a little gallery in the main alley and we've decided to go in and ask the price. It's a stylised version of Monemvasia, almost a caricature, a fitting souvenir of the Peloponnese, we hope.

The man we assume is the artist is seated behind the small counter in the gallery, a short, stocky man of about seventy with longish thick wavy white hair and a bushy moustache, everyone's idea of what a Greek artist should look like. He's watching BBC World News on a laptop and a cigarette is burning in an ashtray on the counter. His name, according to all the art on view, is Manolis Gregoreas, born in Athens but having lived on the Rock for the last twenty-five years. The poster, he says, is thirty euros and he will include a cardboard tube so that we can get it home safely. We're happy with the price and hand over the cash.

"Where are you from?" he asks as he gives us the poster in its protective tube, and when we tell him he refers us to his laptop screen. He has been watching live coverage of the latest terrorist attack in the UK, the fourth or fifth incident so far this year, although, mercifully, this bombing of a London Underground train has not resulted in any deaths.

"It is terrible," he says, clearly upset by what he has been watching. "It cannot go on. Someone will have to pay for it." We nod our agreement and leave him to his thoughts.

CHAPTER FIVE

Neapoli – No ice cream or pizzas

We've spent a long time trying to work out the best way to reach our next destination, Neapoli, which is the birthplace of neither multi-coloured ice cream nor the pizza but a little port town at the tip of the Laconia peninsula whose main purpose in life seems to be to serve the island of Kythira, a few kilometres offshore. We'd assumed before we got to Monemvasia that there'd be a bus service between the two places, but we were told almost as soon as we arrived in Gefyra that that wasn't an option. On the map it appears to be no more than about forty kilometres away, tantalisingly close, but if we are to continue travelling only on public transport, we're going to have to cover more than twice that distance. We will have to take the bus back towards Sparta, get off in the little village of Molai about forty kilometres along the road, then wait for the bus from Sparta to Neapoli. And wait not just for a few minutes, not even for half an hour, but for as much as six hours.

We've passed through Molai when we came to Gefyra a few days ago. The bus station, a kiosk on a gravelly car park, is on the outskirts of the village, at the foot of a steepish hill. Even if we wanted to spend six hours there, it appeared that we wouldn't be able to store our luggage anywhere while we walked up into the village. And when we were in the village would we find a taverna or two where we could while away a few hours? We looked online and couldn't find anywhere.

We talked to Giorgios when we returned to Mpalkoni after our final meal in Gefyra last night, and after mulling over the options, and wondering why we hadn't hired a car for this journey, he recommended that we take a taxi. It would be quick and simple, he said, and it wouldn't cost us any more than fifty euros. Given our avowed intent to do the whole thing using only buses and ferries, it seemed a little like cheating, but we told ourselves we'd done well getting this far on public transport and that one taxi ride would be permissible. After all, weren't taxis a form of public transport? And we calculated that fifty euros wasn't much more than the bus fares we'd have to pay.

And so, after breakfast on another still sunny morning, we drag our bags down Mpalkoni's steep stairs to the street and walk down to the corner where a couple of taxis normally park. The one at the front, a smart newish-looking Mercedes, is empty, but the driver of the second shouts to a colleague sitting outside a café across the street. A tall good-looking shaven-headed man of about forty in shorts and a bright white tee-shirt crosses the street towards us.

"Neapoli," I say. "How much?"

"Forty-five euros."

"OK. That's fine."

He places our bags carefully in the boot of the Merc, then opens the rear passenger doors and gestures for us to get in, shutting the doors gently behind us. We sink into the leather upholstery and enjoy one of the most comfortable rides we've had in weeks. The driver says nothing throughout the forty-five-minute ride across the beautiful mountains of southern Laconia, on roads that are often single track and unevenly surfaced, until we reach the outskirts of Neapoli, when he asks where we're staying.

"Neapoli Rooms." He shakes his head, clearly never having heard of it. It doesn't matter. As we turn out of a side street onto the seafront, we spot a gleaming white modern four-storey building on our left, a board outside announcing that it is Neapoli Rooms. The taxi screeches to a halt and our driver lifts our bags from its boot and places them on the top step at the front of the building. I take a fifty-euro note from my wallet and the driver starts to fish for change in his bum bag.

"That's fine," I tell him. "We don't need the change." He smiles broadly, shakes my hand, wishes us a happy stay and drives off.

Almost before we're aware, a middle-aged woman has appeared at the door. She doesn't speak much English, but Barbara has an email and our hostess is happy that we're who we say we are. She shows us to a room on the first floor, small but spotless, with a large balcony and opposite the beach with a view along the seafront to the ferry terminal. More than adequate for the single night we plan to stay here.

*

Home to around three thousand people, Neapoli, or 'New Town', is little more than a seafront strip with a nice-looking beach and more than its fair share of tavernas and bars. "Uninspiring", according to our guidebook, but popular with Greek holidaymakers. We don't expect to hear too much English being spoken. We make ourselves a cup of tea, wander along the seafront to the ferry office and buy tickets for tomorrow morning's crossing to Kythira, then settle down at one of the harbourside tavernas for lunch. There's apparently been a settlement on this site since the tenth century BC, but it was destroyed by an earthquake in the fourth century AD and only laid out again in its present form in the nineteenth century, when a German architect clearly lacking in imagination gave it the name of New Town.

After a long and leisurely lunch, we return to Neapoli Rooms to soak up the afternoon sunshine on our spacious balcony. People are swimming, walking along the seafront, lying on the beach, enjoying the beautiful afternoon in their own relaxed way. It's a little after seven-thirty when a KTEL bus passes beneath our balcony on its way towards the centre of the town, the bus we would have been arriving on had we chosen that option, seven hours after we got here in our taxi. As we savour the chilled rosé wine we've just bought in a nearby supermarket, we feel more than a little self-satisfied.

And it's while we're enjoying our pre-prandial drink that I suddenly get the sense that the building next to ours houses a very seedy nightclub. I'm looking around, admiring the view as the sun begins to set over the island of Elafonissos to our left, when my eyes are drawn to a sign on the neighbouring block, part of which is visible above our balcony wall. In large bright red lettering on an illuminated white background I can read the words "Hot Arse".

Slightly shocked, I turn to Barbara. "Have you seen what's next door?"

She looks, then almost chokes on a mouthful of rosé. "Oh my gosh," she exclaims. "Where have we come?"

I put my glass on the table and stand up, and as I do so the whole of the sign becomes visible. "Hotel Arsenakos", it reads, with "Rooms available" in smaller lettering underneath.

We look at each other and collapse in fits of laughter.

*

Despite its "uninspiring" tag, we like Neapoli and its more than adequate allocation of tavernas. We enjoy an excellent dinner on the harbourside, only slightly marred by an American/Greek couple loudly Skyping family back home in the USA, before returning to our accommodation to spend a pleasant hour on the balcony in the warm late-evening air.

Chapter Six

Kythira – "Sorry, we're closed"

The morning ferry to Kythira, the *Porfyrousa*, is due to leave at nine and we're there in plenty of time. It gives us the opportunity to find a vantage point on the upper deck, from where we can watch as the crew cram as many vehicles as possible onto the open car deck below, many of whose occupants choose to stay in their cars and vans throughout the crossing. It's quite an achievement by the crew. Just as it seems that they can't possibly accommodate another vehicle, a car drives up the ramp, others are moved around like dominoes being shuffled and the latecomer is fitted in. And while all this is going on several massive trucks are loaded onto the enclosed lower deck where we've left our luggage.

The *Porfyrousa* leaves Neapoli on the stroke of nine o'clock, the sea is flat calm and within little more than an hour we're approaching Kythira's main port of Diakofti, where we're staying for the next two nights. As we near the harbour we're struck by the disconcerting sight of a shipwreck just offshore, the bow of a Dutch cargo ship that ran aground in 2000 sticking up at a forty-five-degree angle, left there as a warning to other shipping. The port was developed just over twenty years ago on a little island called Makrokythira and linked to the main island by a causeway, across which the cars, vans and trucks now head. We stand on the quayside and wonder what to do next.

When we book accommodation on an island and arrive by ferry we normally email or text in advance and ask if someone can meet us at the port. Greek ferry terminals are often quite a distance from town or village centres, accommodation tucked up back streets that aren't always easy to find. When we get an answer it's generally an offer to meet us. Sometimes someone comes to meet us even when we haven't asked. This time, for what reason we're not quite sure, we've forgotten to ask and we appear to be a long way from anywhere. There's a single building on the quayside where other foot passengers from the ferry are picking up hire cars, but no sign of a taxi and nothing that says "This way to the village centre". But there's only one road across the causeway and there are some buildings a kilometre or so away that we assume make up Diakofti, so we set off on foot.

It's hot now as we approach the centre of the day, necessitating numerous stops for water along the way, and it takes us almost an hour to reach the cluster of buildings on the island. The accommodation we've booked, Filoxenes Katoikies, is beside the road leading from the port to the rest of the island and our young landlord Andreas is in his office on the ground floor. When he realises we've walked from the ferry he apologises profusely for not having come to collect us.

"I thought you would hire a car, most people do," he says in almost flawless English, leading us to assume that he must at some point have lived in the UK. "You will be able to hire one here. You will probably need it."

"No buses?" I ask, feeling let down once again by a guidebook that has suggested there is at least a limited amount of public transport.

Andreas shakes his head. "No, not anymore," he says. "But I can take you around the island. There's a very good restaurant at Avlemonas if you would like to go."

"There's a taverna here in Diakofti?" I ask. "I thought we passed one just down the road."

"Afraid not," says Andreas. "Not at the moment anyway. They are in dispute over the land they use outside the restaurant. They are prevented from opening until the dispute is settled by the court. We hope they will open some time soon but no one knows." And then, "Follow me."

He picks up both of our bags and leads us round to the back of the building and up two flights of stairs to the door of our accommodation. He's red-faced and sweating. "I must give up smoking," he says, smiling. "Where are you from in England?" he asks as he opens the door and lets us in to a large bright room.

We tell him. "I was at university in Guildford for three years," he says.

"So you know Brighton?" I ask.

"Sadly, no," Andreas replies. "I never went there. My family has several holiday places here on Kythira. When I finished my studies, I came back here to help run the business. Now I'm married with a baby, so I guess I'll stay."

He leaves us to do some unpacking, returning about five minutes later with the gift of a delicious-looking sponge cake topped with desiccated coconut and made by his wife. There's a minimarket a few metres along the street, he says, and a place where we can hire a car, and if we need him he'll be in the office downstairs.

*

Despite its location off the southern tip of the Peloponnese, Kythira belongs to the Ionian group of islands and is administered from Corfu, which right now seems a million miles away. In 2006 there was an earthquake whose epicentre was only a few kilometres off the island, an information board near the land end of the causeway tells us. One person on Kythira was injured and "several" buildings and roads were damaged. It is also Greece's seventeenth-largest island, notes the board, and the place where Aphrodite was supposedly born. But in truth there isn't a great deal to its main port. There are houses, mostly modern, and small apartment blocks scattered over a relatively wide area, but since Diakofti caters largely for Greek weekenders and it's currently Thursday it's pretty quiet. What happened to all the cars that were crammed onto the ferry's deck earlier is anyone's guess.

The minimarket that Andreas has promised us will be open is about fifty metres along a dirt road from our accommodation, and the car hire office is in the Maistrali Apartments just behind it. Both appear to be deserted. An elderly man is seated on a kitchen chair in the shade of the shop's awning.

"When does the shop open?" I ask.

"Later," he replies gruffly. "Maybe five or six." It's just turned three o'clock.

We wander off down the dirt road towards the deserted beach, linger for a few minutes at the water's edge, then head back. The old man has gone now but even from the middle of the road we're aware of some movement in the shop. We press our noses to the window and within seconds the door opens and a small middle-aged woman welcomes us inside. Her name is Nota, she tells us, and she has so many things to do today that she can't have the shop open all the time. If it's closed next time we need anything we should go around the back and ask for her.

It's dark and dingy and far from being the best-stocked shop we've ever seen, but it does have the essentials – wine, beer, eggs and bread. We buy enough to keep us going for a while and thank Nota for her kindness. Outside, we notice that the door to the car rental office is now open so we venture inside. Filippos, who appears to double up as the local car and boat mechanic, greets us warmly, tells us that his small cars cost twenty euros a day and he'll be at our accommodation at ten in the morning with the relevant paperwork. If we have cash it would be better.

After showering and changing – and emailing Neapoli Rooms and asking if we can go back there in two nights' time – we take up Andreas's offer of a lift to Avlemonas. It's a short if spectacular drive, no more than fifteen or twenty minutes up a steepish twisting road out of Diakofti and onto a mountain plateau, where we're treated to the sight of long-horned mountain goats grazing at the roadside, then down another narrow winding road to the picturesque seaside village. Sotiris, a highly recommended fish taverna, sits above the picturesque little harbour, sheltered from the rather fierce wind that has developed since we arrived on the island. We're invited to choose our fish from the kitchen, and we enjoy another excellent meal in tranquil surroundings before I text Andreas and ask him to come and pick us up.

*

The wind that had been howling most of the night has dropped, although the downside is that it's overcast and by ten o'clock, when Filippos knocks on our door with the keys to a Nissan Micra and some compulsory paperwork, it's begun to rain.

"Don't worry," says Filippos, indicating a patch of blue sky that appears to be approaching Diakofti. "Maybe ten or fifteen minutes, it will stop." We thank him for his optimism, sign a couple of forms and hand over a twenty-euro note. The only instruction he gives us is that we should top up the tank at the end of the day.

He proves to be right about the weather. As we head up to the plateau and across the island towards the capital Chora the rain stops and it becomes a bright morning. We pass the airport, expanded extensively in the early part of this century, largely with private funds from the locals, so that it now receives a daily flight from Athens, and within an hour are in the back streets of Chora looking for a parking space. Sadly, the sunny weather hasn't lasted. A mist has rolled in over the island and it's cool and breezy.

Perched on a rock above the seaside village of Kapsali, Chora is a maze of narrow alleyways lined with whitewashed houses. Most of them lead up to the Venetian Kastro, the thirteenth-century castle which has been allowed to fall into genteel disrepair without too much restoration work and which normally affords stunning views over the little island of Hytra. Normally, since today's view of the rock, also known as Avgo (the 'Egg') that is one of the reputed birthplaces of Aphrodite, is severely restricted by the mist. Chora's main square, Plateia Dimitriou Stai, is planted with hibiscus, bougainvillea and palms and is undoubtedly pretty and after our exertions of scrambling over the castle's ruins we relax for a while with a cup of coffee.

A little like Diakofti, we can't find a taverna that's open at lunchtime. Instead, we drive back up the island for ten kilometres until we come to the little town of Livadi and find Pierro's taverna on the main street, a restaurant that's been highly recommended by Andreas. It doesn't disappoint. As we enter the large dining room we're greeted by a genial middle-aged Greek we assume to be Pierro who treats us like members of his family. He shows us to a table, brings us a bottle of water which he says is "on the house," then invites us into the kitchen, where three smiling women are tending to a collection of large pans on the stove. Pierro describes the contents of each and the way they've been prepared and cooked as if he has done all the work himself.

As we eat our lunch, accompanied by a half-litre of house red wine, he comes to our table from time to time, ostensibly to ask how we are enjoying the food but taking the opportunity at each visit to ask about our travels and tell us about his time in England. He has cousins in London, he tells us. He likes England and would like to have settled there, but his wife is from Kythira and doesn't want to leave, even though their children have moved to the mainland. But he's happy. He has his taverna and his friends and he is always meeting new people – "like yourselves." Remarkably, the meal comes to exactly twenty euros, although Pierro gives us neither bill nor receipt. A real Greek experience.

*

Since Filippos has asked us to top up the Micra's tank, our next brief stop has to be at a petrol station. A map we've picked up shows that the only one in this part of the island is a few kilometres outside Livadi on the main road back towards Diakofti and within minutes we're pulling onto the forecourt. A young man comes out of the building and attempts to operate one of his three pumps. We don't know why but it isn't working. He goes inside, then emerges again and tries a second pump, again without success. We move forward a couple of metres to the third pump and the young man tries again. Eventually he hangs up the nozzle, goes inside, then re-emerges looking apologetic.

"I'm sorry," he says. "We don't have any gas." It shouldn't be a problem – the tank's still almost full.

In what must be almost the dead geographical centre of the island, surrounded by wild, open countryside, we come across a smart new supermarket. Not much bigger than a Tesco Metro but a modern supermarket, nevertheless. Given its location, it's almost certainly the only supermarket on Kythira. We'd been wondering what we'd do for dinner this evening, being reluctant to ask Andreas to act as our chauffeur again. Problem solved. The shelves are well stocked and within minutes we've got the ingredients for a meal that can easily be prepared with the limited amount of equipment in our studio – and we've got the sponge cake for dessert.

When we get back down into Diakofti there's no sign of Filippos at his office. We scribble a note explaining that we weren't able to buy any petrol, leave it on the driver's seat along with ten euros that we feel should easily cover the amount of fuel we've used and pop the car keys through the letter box. He knows where we are if he feels we've tried to cheat him.

*

We haven't wasted our second and final evening on Kythira, even though we've been confined to our studio and its balcony. We've used the iPad to plan the remainder of our time on the Peloponnese, to search bus timetables and to book accommodation. When we leave the island later today, we'll have another overnight stay in Neapoli before getting a bus back to Sparta and another to Gythio, the 'capital' of the Mani, the remote, barren peninsula so beloved of Patrick Leigh Fermor and so little explored by visitors to Greece. After a couple of days we plan to move on again, this time deeper into the Mani to Areopoli, which our guidebook describes as the "last bit of civilisation before the Deep Mani". And then we'll move north, to the picturesque seaside village of Stoupa where we spent a week over ten years ago, before heading to Kalamata and picking up a long-distance bus to Athens.

After breakfast we wander downstairs to the office to settle our bill with Andreas.

"I have a gift for you," he says after his card machine has accepted our payment. He opens a drawer in his desk and takes out a clear plastic bag of salt weighing about a kilogram. "Kythira sea salt," he adds. "The best... What time does your ferry leave?"

Less than fifteen minutes before departure time Andreas loads our luggage into the rear end of his small hatchback, the larger of our bags hanging precariously out of the back. He drives slowly and carefully across the causeway, veering from side to side to avoid the potholes that could jar the car and deposit the bag, a kilogram heavier than it was when we arrived on the island, on the road. He leaves us on the quayside and wishes us well, and we've barely had time to find seats on the open deck before the ferry pulls away. Within two hours we're back in the same small room at Neapoli Rooms that we had three days ago, having been warmly welcomed back by the same friendly woman. Disappointingly, Kythira has been not much more than an island-grab – but we would have kicked ourselves and wondered 'what if?' if we hadn't been.

CHAPTER SEVEN

Gythio – "The greatest seduction of all time"

When we went to the bus depot yesterday afternoon to buy tickets for this morning's journey to Gythio, the woman behind the counter asked where we were staying. It wasn't just a friendly question.

"Does the bus leave from here?" I'd asked.

"Don't worry," the woman replied. "I will ask the driver to stop at your hotel. It will be just after eight o'clock."

And so here we are, at eight o'clock, on the pavement outside Neapoli Rooms with our landlady waiting with us to wave us off. And, as promised, at five past the bus comes into view around a bend about a hundred metres away and pulls up beside us. The smiling driver jumps down from his seat, loads our bags into the luggage hold, then waits until we're settled before pulling away again. Just over two hours later we're back at the bus station in Sparta. It's heaving with young people and we have to elbow our way through to the ticket office window to buy our tickets for Gythio. But the ancient bus that's due to leave in ten minutes' time is almost empty and only two or three other couples accompany us on the forty-five-kilometre journey down to the Gulf of Laconia.

Gythio is known as the capital of the Mani, once a bustling port town with a neoclassical harbour-front and a harbour that all too sadly contains too many rusting, unused hulks. It was a wealthy town in Roman times, exporting the purple molluscs that were used for dyeing togas, and until the Second World War exported acorns used in leather-tanning. We've booked a room at the Hotel Aktaion, a few minutes' walk along the seafront from where the bus stops, a smart building in Venetian style that a leaflet we pick up in reception tells us was renovated in 1995 and is "the most beautiful building in Gythio." According to our guidebook "inside, it doesn't live up to its grand exterior, but it's pleasant enough". Since we left Sparta the sky has grown steadily darker and more threatening and as we unpack a few things in our small but perfectly adequate room we hear rumbles of thunder in the distance. The wind begins to toss small boats up and down in the harbour and heavy spots of rain start to batter our French window.

We wait half an hour until the rain dies down, then walk a short distance along the seafront until we find Barba Sideris, the one taverna that makes it into the guidebook and where we get delicious roast pork served on wax paper in a lunch that costs less than twenty euros in total. But when we leave and begin to scour the streets for a minimarket that's not having an afternoon break – I've run out of deodorant – the heavens open again. Roads turn into rivers, flights of steps become waterfalls, torrents cascade down from shop awnings. Flashes of lightning and cracks of thunder add to what is one of the worst storms we've ever experienced in Greece. We dart from shop doorway to taverna canopy until we find a store that's open and selling what we need, then take a similarly evasive course back to the hotel to dry out.

It's dry and much brighter when we go out for dinner. We find Trata on the old harbour, a traditional family-run taverna where we get excellent service and simple tasty food and a bill for just over twenty-two euros. It's quiet, almost deserted, when we go back to the Aktaion, a little chilly but dry, and the forecast for tomorrow is good.

*

It's a warm sunny morning with no hint of the cloud that hung over Gythio for most of yesterday. We've slept well and enjoyed a good buffet breakfast in the hotel and are now setting out to explore what there is of interest in this attractive little town. Mythology has it that the town was founded by the unlikely pairing of Heracles and Apollo, and that the little island of Kranae, less than a hundred metres offshore, was described by Homer as the site of Paris and Helen of Troy's first night together after they had escaped from her husband, King Menelaus of Sparta, in what was called one of the greatest seductions of all time. Then, as now, Gythio was the main port for Sparta, and after their night of passion the lovers fled by ship to Troy. By all accounts Menelaus was seriously miffed, but generations of poets and storytellers continue to be grateful.

Kranae is now known as Marathonisi and is connected to the mainland by a concrete mole or causeway, across which we walk after our five-euro buffet breakfast in the Aktaion. The once-bare island has been planted with fir trees by the local authority and it has a truly romantic atmosphere. There's a lighthouse on the southern tip of the island, but our real destination is the eighteenth-century Tzanetakis Grigorakis Tower housing a small museum relating to the history of the Mani through the eyes of European travellers from the fifteenth to the nineteenth centuries. "Worth its low and oddly specific entry price (€1.47)" says the guidebook. "The one drawback is that the museum is often closed when it shouldn't be." Like this morning. We follow the advice to knock on what is supposed to be the office door at the corner of the building but get no response, there are no opening hours posted anywhere and to be honest the place looks as if it hasn't been open for some time. No wonder Paris and Helen only stayed one night!

A twenty-minute walk along Akti Vasileos Pavlou, the seafront road, to the opposite end of the town and into the back streets, following the indicator signs, brings us to Gythio's other site of historical interest, the Ancient Theatre. At least, we assume it's of historical interest. We can't find any information about it anywhere, not in our guidebook or online. It's basically a few tiers of stone seats arranged in a semi-circle and seriously overgrown. There are no information boards and, as such, no clue as to how 'ancient' it actually is. There's a dusty car park which doesn't look as if it's been used in months and a high barbed-wire-topped fence that separates the theatre from an army base, the whole site being overlooked by a heavily overgrown acropolis. But apart from the time it takes to get a few photographs, there isn't much point in lingering. Gythio is an attractive little town, although there isn't much more to it than Akti Vasileos Pavlou and the squares at each end. Having been to Marathonisi and the Ancient Theatre, we feel we've seen it all, and we spend the rest of our time in the town enjoying the hospitality of the local bars and tavernas.

Chapter Eight

Areopoli – "Just choose which room you want"

The bus that will take us on the shortest leg of our travels around the Peloponnese doesn't leave until lunchtime, so we spend the last few hours of our short stay in Gythio sitting outside various cafés and bars and indulging in some serious people-watching. A sign outside one of the local pharmacies says it's twenty-nine degrees at 11am, another a few doors away tells us it's twenty-five. We assume it's somewhere in between, a more than comfortable temperature for sitting outside and watching the world go by. We haven't come across any native English-speakers for some time now and we're struck by the number of large motorhomes that have made it here from northern Europe. Most of them have French or German registration plates, but there's a sprinkling of Belgian and Dutch. Coming here by road must be something of an adventure and, without expensive cross-Channel ferries, flights and hotels to pay for, clearly an economical way of doing it. But the thought of having to empty a chemical toilet every morning doesn't really appeal.

We arrive in Areopoli at around one-thirty, at a proper bus station with a large car park, a café and a booking office. It's beside the main road down the Mani, surrounded by supermarkets, new houses and a garage and we immediately begin to wonder whether we've made a good decision. But as we cross the road the little town becomes increasingly prettier and more traditionally Maniot, all winding cobbled streets and handsome stone tower houses. Areopoli was originally known as Tzimova but in the nineteenth century the locals adopted the name Areopoli, from Ares, the Greek god of war. It was here in March 1821 that Maniot clan chiefs united under the local leader Petrobey Mavromihalis in opposition to the Ottoman occupation. The small army marched north, gathering followers on the way and eventually capturing Kalamata. Thus the Greek War of Independence began.

To honour this cradle of independence, Areopoli's main square is Platea 17 Martiou (March 17th), dominated by a massive statue of Petrobey Mavromihalis, a truly fearsome-looking individual who must have commanded the respect of all his followers and struck fear into the hearts of any Turk who opposed him.

Fifty metres away, opposite the little twin churches of Panagios and Agios Haralambos, we find Fivos Studios, up half a dozen stone steps from street level. It's an impressive stone building dating from the late nineteenth century but restored a couple of years ago. The front door is open – not just unlocked but wide open – but there's no one around. On the website we'd used to book it a couple of previous visitors had complained that there was no one there to greet them when they arrived, and they'd recommended scouring the local bars asking for the landlord. We take what we believe is the easier option and phone the number on the sign on the wall next to the door.

"Go upstairs and choose which room you want," a man's voice tells us. "We'll talk later."

There are four doors on the lower floor, all of which appear to be locked. At the top of a steep flight of stairs are three studios, all with open doors. The one we'd most like, a spacious room with a view over the street, has an unmade bed and a half-full waste bin in the bathroom, both of which we assume will be seen to when the landlord or a cleaner arrives. We leave our bags in the hall and go up to a taverna near the main square for gyros and a jug of wine.

When we go back to Fivos three quarters of an hour later there's still no sign of the landlord and no indication that anyone's been there since we phoned. I call again.

"I'll be there in five minutes."

Ten minutes later my phone rings with a call from a different number and I explain our problem. We've chosen a room but it hasn't been cleaned since the last guests were there.

"OK. Someone will be there soon."

It doesn't sound promising but within minutes a woman with very limited English appears and tells us to take our pick – they have no other guests at the moment. She opens the doors on the ground floor to reveal a large, three-bedroom apartment with a suntrap of a terrace that's almost large enough to play five-a-side football on, and we ask if we can have it.

She smiles and nods. "No more money," she says. "You can stay here."

We have dinner at O Poulis, almost next door to Fivos, served by a charming young Greek woman who speaks flawless English and delivers excellent if a little Westernised food. She chats with us between courses, the usual topic of where we're from and what we're doing. Of all the foreign many tourists who come here, she tells us, the French are the least popular with the locals. We wonder why.

"Because they won't speak English!"

*

It's a beautiful peaceful morning and all we can hear as we sit on our spacious terrace is the sound of birdsong and the occasional rumble of a truck on the main road. A dog barks every now and then but it's so infrequent it doesn't even irritate. It's not all paradise, however. We can't get the cooker to work. After we'd finally settled in, I'd received a message from the landlord (we never discovered his name) telling me to text him if we had any problems. I do, but since we've no idea how long it might be until I get a response, we look for alternative solutions. In one of the studios upstairs there's a little two-ring hob plugged into the wall by the sink. (The front door has been wedged open all night, the studios unlocked. Back in Brighton we would almost certainly have had squatters for neighbours by now.) The hob is easily disconnected, carried downstairs and used to cook our breakfast before the woman who let us in yesterday and a man we assume to be the landlord arrive. Solving our problem is a question of flicking all the fuse switches off and on again until the red light that indicates the cooker is now working comes on. The man asks politely if everything else is OK, then they leave.

Back at the bus station we take the noon service to Gerolimenas – ourselves, a young Australian woman who's travelling around Greece on her own and who we've bumped into once or twice before, and four locals. There's nothing we particularly want to see or do when we get there. It's just that Gerolimenas is as deep into the Mani as you can reach on public transport, you probably need a donkey cart to go much further, so we have to go. And it's a wonderful journey through some beautiful desolate countryside, a land that's known as the Bad Mountains, dotted with stone tower houses in various states of repair, from the derelict to the recently renovated. Isolated churches blend into the dusty hills. It's a wild, inhospitable landscape where nothing of value grows, supposedly sparsely populated by a wild, war-like breed of men with thick shoulder-length black hair. We silently wish that the bus doesn't break down.

It doesn't, of course, and after about an hour and a half it drops down into the seaside village of Gerolimenas – and we are immediately taken aback by its beauty. A small horseshoe-shaped bay hemmed in on three sides by dry brown hills, a handful of little fishing boats bobbing on a crystal-clear sea, a row of tavernas along a pebble beach. We settle down at one of them, Akrotainartis, and enjoy a leisurely lunch – because there isn't really anything else to do. Inside, there's a small framed poster on one of the walls claiming that Patrick Leigh Fermor stayed there while he was researching and writing *Mani*. He devoted several pages to Gerolimenas, clearly as smitten as everyone else who sees it. "Yerolimena" Leigh Fermor called it, claiming that it had once been a major port where steamers from Athens regularly called. During the late nineteenth century the port was exporting seven thousand quails a month to France, but the twentieth century saw a slow decline in its fortunes. The upgrade of the roads on the Mani from dirt tracks to tarmacked surfaces has meant that this pretty little village has become a popular weekend getaway destination for Athenians although today, in the middle of the week, it's quiet and it's difficult to imagine it any other way.

This evening, our last in Areopoli, we walk down to the old square for dinner at Barba Petros, the one restaurant in the village recommended by our guidebook. It's a strange experience. We're the only diners there but the woman who serves us, even though she invites us into the kitchen to choose our food, doesn't seem overly keen on having our custom. Good food, and inexpensive, but rather like eating in a funeral parlour. Outside a bar near our studios a group of local men are watching football on a big screen. There's silence as PAOK Thessaloniki go two-one up against local favourites Panathinaikos, then shouts of encouragement as the Athens team makes a spirited fight back. Otherwise, Areopoli has pretty much turned in for the night.

CHAPTER NINE

Stoupa – "Free wine for life"

In the bus station at Areopoli you really feel as if you're travelling. It's a large dusty gravel area marked with parking bays and with a proper ticket office and a café in one corner. We buy our tickets for Stoupa ("Change at Itylo," we're told by the woman behind the desk) and a couple of cold drinks from the café and settle down on a bench outside to wait for the bus. And then there's drama. In the café there's the sound of furniture being knocked over and it appears that an elderly man has collapsed as he's tried to stand up. Several people have sprung to his aid and a woman we assume to be the café manager has rushed outside shouting into her mobile phone. Within minutes there's the wail of a siren and an ambulance from the village's medical centre swings onto the car park and screeches to a halt outside the café. Shortly afterwards, the man is helped outside and into the ambulance by the paramedics. He's on his feet but extremely unsteady so hopefully he's not too ill, and he appears to be complaining about being taken to the medical centre.

The bus for the first leg of our journey to Itylo leaves on time at two and apart from a handful of schoolchildren we're the only passengers. It goes up and down along some picturesque coastline until it stops about fifteen minutes later with just us and a boy of about twelve still on board. The driver turns to us, then points to a stone bench under an expansive tree and says, "One hour." The boy is met by his mother and driven off. The bus driver unloads our bags and wishes us "Goodbye," then performs a three-point turn in the road and heads back towards Areopoli, leaving us alone. Apart from the bench, there's a small brick building about the size of a garden shed that doesn't look as if it's been used for some years but was no doubt at one time the bus station. Under the tree there's a flatbed truck laden with all manner of fruit and vegetables and a pair of feet in shabby trainers hanging out of the window on the passenger's side. Beside the truck a man of about fifty with untidy hair and a bushy greying moustache is asleep on a dirty rug. He snores and grunts and turns over so he has his back to us, clearly not wanting to be disturbed.

We're not actually in Itylo but on a road that runs above the village, which we can see through the trees about a kilometre away, a crumbling and tranquil backwater according to our guidebook. We could probably walk down to the centre easily enough and get lunch but in the heat of the afternoon sun we don't fancy the climb back up to the road hauling our luggage behind us. There are, apparently, two cafés somewhere in the vicinity of the bus stop, but we don't see any sign of them. We've got a packet of biscuits in one of our bags and there's a communal tap next to the tree dispensing cool drinking water. It's a peaceful spot, the silence only broken by the singing of the birds, the occasional French motorhome and the snores of the man on the rug. We both take out the books we're currently reading and settle down on the bench for a quiet hour. Why would we want to be anywhere else?

At one point about half an hour in the man on the rug wakes, helps himself to an apple from the back of the truck, scoffs it greedily, smokes a roll-up cigarette and turns over and goes back to sleep again. He appears not to be disturbed by the arrival of a group of about ten middle-aged Italians on motorbikes. They're all in black leathers and some have white hair that most people would consider too long for men of their age. They fill up their water bottles from the tap, several of them enjoy a quick cigarette, before they all remount and ride off in the direction of Stoupa.

As the end of the hour draws near people begin to appear, mostly in cars which they park around the tree and in which they remain, presumably waiting to meet someone on the incoming bus. A number of others have walked up from the village carrying parcels that the bus driver will deliver for them. The hour passes and people start to get agitated, looking at their watches every few minutes. Greek buses are almost invariably late so they shouldn't really worry. It eventually arrives about twenty minutes behind schedule, disgorges all its passengers, makes a quick turn in the road and heads back towards Kalamata, an elderly woman, us and the two-man crew the only people on board.

It's a spectacular ride up to Stoupa, the sea down below on our left-hand side, the mountains rearing up on the right. We thread through little villages on roads barely wide enough to take the bus, like thick cotton through the eye of a small needle. We inch around precarious-looking hairpin bends. We go up and down steep slopes. We divert from the main road to pass through the little fishing village of Agios Nikolaos before, after about an hour, we find ourselves on the outskirts of Stoupa. The bus doesn't go into the centre of the village, the roads are too narrow, but instead drops us outside a supermarket on the main road, across the road from which is the accommodation we booked while we were in Gythio, Elena Apartments. We're greeted by a lovely bubbly middle-aged woman we assume to be Elena herself and shown into our spacious well-equipped studio. She's even pre-tuned the television to BBC World News.

Down on the seafront, a couple of hundred metres away, it seems much more developed than when we were here in 2005, more roads have been surfaced, more blocks of holiday accommodation built on the side streets. The small studio complex overlooking the Kalogria beach where we stayed then has been demolished and replaced with a hotel. And almost all we hear are English voices. We've heard a fair amount of English being spoken since we've been on the Peloponnese but it's largely been Europeans from other countries talking to the locals. Stoupa seems to have become something of a British enclave, the sort of place where you hear the Brits complain that there are 'too many foreigners' here, but it is still very pretty and as we sit and enjoy our dinner at the Five Brothers taverna on the seafront we're treated to a most amazing sunset that compensates for a great deal.

*

It's a beautiful morning, made even sunnier just after nine when there's a knock at our studio door and a smiling Elena presents us with half a dozen eggs. We haven't seen any chickens around, but the supermarket is just across the road and it's a lovely kind gesture. We've decided to take the short bus ride up the coast to Kardamyli, said to have one of the most perfect settings of any Greek village and a place that clearly captivated Leigh Fermor. He visited the village several times before building a house there in the 1960s and staying there until he died in 2011.

Already waiting at the bus stop is a group of OAPs from West Yorkshire, four couples, laughing loudly, calling each other silly names and generally behaving like a class of eight-year-olds on a school trip. It's like *Last of the Summer Wine* on tour. In one slightly more serious moment a debate grows about a tree next to the bus stop, a fragrant specimen with a plethora of blue trumpet-shaped flowers and fern-like leaves. Various possible names are offered until one of the women turns to Barbara.

"What do you think it is, love?" she asks.

Barbara looks more closely. "I think it's a jacaranda."

"Thanks, love," says the woman, then turning back to her friends, "this lady says it's a, what did you say love, a Jackanory." They fall about like children in the playground who've just heard a rather risqué joke.

The journey to Kardamyli takes twenty minutes and costs one euro twenty each. We leave the bus and make our way up a gentle slope into the historic and carefully restored old town, stopping in our tracks at the sight of a small owl perched on top of a street lamp. We eye each other suspiciously for a few seconds, then slowly approach with the intention of taking a photograph. Sadly, the owl's having nothing of it and he flies off to a nearby rooftop and watches us carefully as we continue our walk into the old town.

This was the private compound of the powerful Troupakis-Mourtzinos family, a once imposing fortress built in the seventeenth century and enclosing the Byzantine church of Agios Spiridon and the Mourtzinos Tower, once occupied by the head of the powerful Troupakis clan. The buildings next to the tower have been converted into a museum as recently as 2005, part of a network that illustrates day-to-day life in the Mani. It's small but contains some interesting exhibits and the entire site has been carefully restored to give an impression of what life may have been like when the clan leaders held court here in the eighteenth and nineteenth centuries.

After an hour or so clambering over ruins and climbing up and down stone stairs we've worked up a thirst. We wander back down into the new village, a largely ribbon development strung out along both sides of the main road, and find our way to Lela's. The eponymous Lela was Leigh Fermor's housekeeper and apparently produced beautiful classical Greek food for twenty-five years until she died in 2015. We sit on the terrace and enjoy the beautiful view across the Messinian Gulf with our cold beers.

*

On the way from our accommodation to the seafront, there's a bronze bust at the roadside, oddly placed since its subject is looking across the road towards a campsite with his back to the spectacular view over the Kalogria beach and over the Messinian Gulf. On close inspection we can just about read the worn Greek script and identify the rather stern-looking man. It's Nikos Kazantzakis, the writer best known outside Greece for his novel *Zorba the Greek*. He lived in Stoupa for a while in 1917 and based the central character of his novel on Giorgios Zorbas, a coal mine supervisor in the nearby village of Pastrova. The novel's original title, in Greek, was *The Life and Times of Alexis Zorba*.

It's much quieter this evening, but at the tavernas the tables where you can sit and watch the sunset are occupied from early evening. It's not surprising, the view is pretty special. As we walk along the front, we're approached by a waiter from the taverna Pefka and handed a card offering "Free wine for life". It sounds too good to be true – and it is. But a free half-litre of house wine every time you eat there is an offer not to be sniffed at and since it's in an elevated position at the end of the village and has pretty good views we decide to take it up. Like the taverna's location, the prices are slightly higher than most others, no doubt to compensate for the free wine, but we still get an excellent meal for just over twenty-five euros.

*

We're eating breakfast on our balcony just after ten o'clock when the comparative peace is disturbed by the shrill discordant wailing of sirens on the main road. Because we're shielded from the road by trees we can't see everything that's going on, but we can make out the shapes of several emergency vehicles as they turn off the road and head into Stoupa itself. All goes quiet again, until about fifteen minutes later the sirens blare again. This time two fire engines that look old enough to have seen service in the Second World War plus three ambulances and several other vehicles pull up outside the supermarket next door. They sit there, sirens wailing, for five minutes, doing nothing. No one gets out of any of the vehicles, no one approaches them. Eventually they all pull back onto the road and head off in convoy in the direction of Kardamyli. The wail of the sirens fades and peace is restored.

In the village a little while later we find the Thaneas travel office tucked away in a side street. Seated behind one of the two desks is a small Greek woman of about sixty who looks up from her paperwork, smiles and asks, in flawless English, how she can help.

"Do you sell tickets for KTEL buses?" I ask.

She shakes her head. "I'm afraid not." And then, sensing our disappointment, she asks, "Where do you want to go?"

We explain that we need to get to Athens in a couple of days' time. We think it's probably wisest to try and buy our tickets from Kalamata in advance.

"You should," she agrees. "That service is always busy." And then, "I can buy them for you."

Almost before we know it, she's logged on to the KTEL website and is asking us what time bus we'd like to take. She takes our passports so she can enter our details, then asks for Barbara's credit card and taps away on her keyboard. Within a couple of minutes she's printing out our tickets.

"That's brilliant," I say. "What do we owe you?"

"No charge," she answers with a smile. "What have you guys been doing?" We explain how we've been making our way around various parts of Greece using only buses and ferries. "That's wonderful," she says. "Enjoy yourselves. I love people like you."

We almost run to Agios Nikolaos, the next village three or four kilometres south, so buoyed are we by what that kind woman has done for us and by her comments. It would actually be possible to run now – the footpath that was little more than a rough cart track when we first walked it over a decade ago has since been paved – but it's too hot for anything more strenuous than a brisk walk. The path runs along the clifftop, then after about an hour dips down into the pretty little fishing village, tavernas lined along the seafront and a small fish market that seems to be the focal point of village life. We have a drink at Gregg's – no sausage rolls but an eponymous Australian owner – and lunch at Medusa, where an elderly woman doubles as both chef and waitress and cooks and serves beautiful food, before walking back to Stoupa.

*

On the face of it, Stoupa is little more than a creation of the holiday trade – a very pretty resort but somewhere that has been developed in recent years to meet the needs of tourists from north-west Europe. But it does have some history in the form of a low acropolis at its southern end, the only clue to the village's original existence. It was the site of an ancient city called Leuktra, a name that lives on in Lefktron, a village just inland from here. The acropolis is known rather grandly as Kastro and was the site of a castle built in the thirteenth century following the conquest of the Peloponnese by the Franks and called Beaufort. It's also thought to be the site of a sanctuary of Athena and a small marble bust of the goddess that was found here now resides in the archaeological museum at Kalamata. After breakfast on a beautiful sunny morning we set out to find it.

After following some rather vague directions we eventually find a faded brown signpost bearing the word "Beaufort" and pointing us up an overgrown path towards the top of the hill. It's quite a scramble at times over loose stones and through vegetation that leaves our lower legs covered in small scratches. And when we reach the summit there's nothing left of Beaufort other than a few odd rocks. But the scramble up the hill has been worth it purely for the stunning views up and down the coast, views that make us appreciate once more just how beautiful this part of Greece is.

After taking numerous photographs, we scramble back down again and find ourselves next to a smallholding surrounded by a flimsy wire fence. Which would not normally be a problem were it not for the biggest turkey either of us has ever seen standing no more than five metres away and glaring menacingly. It's the size of an ostrich, and not only is its gaze fixed on us it's making what we can only describe as threatening throaty noises. In my family there was a story of how the elder of my sisters was bundled over by an aggressive turkey in a farmyard when she was about five years old and I've been nervous of them ever since. We risk the monster's wrath by taking a photograph, then turn slowly so as not to alarm it and walk smartly away.

*

The bus stop is barely two minutes from our accommodation, but we're there at least fifteen minutes before the bus to Kalamata is due. Greek buses rarely run to time. Mostly, they're late, of course, but occasionally, very occasionally, they're early and you can't afford to take the chance. As we wait we're joined by several other people who we imagine are locals on their way to work. We have at least four false alarms as buses approach from the direction of Agios Nikolaos. We all step out to the edge of the pavement and stick out our arms, then step back as the buses sail past, full of schoolchildren. We become slightly concerned, as we don't have a great deal of time to make our connection in Kalamata. We're not even sure if the bus we're waiting for goes to the bus station where we pick up the Athens service. And as time passes one or two of the other people waiting also start to get a little agitated. But then it arrives, somewhere between fifteen and thirty minutes late – it's hard to work out precisely how much from the timetable – and everyone's happy.

It's a spectacular journey along the coast road to Kardamyli then up into the mountains, and we make good progress, stopping only at what appears to be the highest point in the area to allow the old man to relieve himself. Just half an hour after leaving Stoupa we can see Kalamata, down below and ahead of us, and for the first time this morning we're confident we'll be able to make the connection.

As the bus weaves through its back streets we realise that Kalamata isn't the prettiest of cities, but it does have an excuse. In the eighties a large earthquake destroyed many of its ancient buildings and much of the city was rebuilt in safe but uninspiring concrete. It was a massive 'quake, apparently, and something of a miracle that only twenty people out of a total population of over forty thousand lost their lives. It's said that at the time of the tremor most of the city was outside watching the inauguration of a new ferry route to Crete. Kalamata is also something of a paradox since it was built on two products at opposite ends of the healthy living scale, two products that typify the Greek lifestyle. At the top of the scale was the product largely believed to be responsible for the good health of Mediterranean people, olive oil. Kalamata oil is recognised the world over as arguably the best. On the other hand, the city has long been home to Karelia, Greece's biggest and best-known brand of cigarettes. Even in these enlightened times, the factory still produces around fifteen billion cigarettes a year.

The bus stops in the city's central square and the passengers file off. We stand, ready to join them.

"You're travelling somewhere else?" a woman who was waiting with us in Stoupa asks.

"Athens," I reply.

"Stay on the bus," she says. "He will take you to the place where you get your connection."

Five minutes later we're in the busy KTEL bus station, ten minutes to spare before our bus is due to leave. It's fully booked and the next one isn't for another couple of hours. We say a silent thank-you to the woman in the travel agency in Stoupa, then settle down to enjoy the three-hour journey to Athens.

PART FOUR

The Dodecanese

Chapter One

Symi – Climbing the stairway to heaven

There can be few more beautiful sights in Greece than the one that greets you at seven-fifteen on a late August evening from the top deck of the Hellenic Seaways' *Nissos Chios* as it cruises into the harbour at Gialos, the main town – the only town – on the little Dodecanese island of Symi. The light at this time of day has that ethereal quality so loved by painters and photographers, picking out the pinks and whites of the houses and churches clustered on the steep sides of the U-shaped bay and making the contrast between the buildings and the arid hillside even starker than usual. Fishing boats bob in the crystal-clear waters of what one guidebook describes as "perhaps the world's prettiest harbour". At first sight, this is a stunningly beautiful place, thanks, it's said, to the Venetians who once ruled the island and established its unique architecture, and after a day's travelling it really is a wonderful sight.

Disembarking is the usual shambles, more chaos than *Chios* as new passengers haul their luggage up the ramp and onto the ship before the leavers have had the chance to get off. We've been told to look out for Andreas (another one!), the son/brother of the mother and daughter who own and run Marina Studios, our home for the next few days. As the crowds thin out we're aware of the presence of a young man in his late twenties, leaning on a moped and holding an A4 sheet of paper above his head, on which the name Barbara is written in pencil. He shakes our hands, takes our bags and gives us directions. Harani Bay, where Marina Studios is situated, is on the opposite tip of the harbour, about two hundred metres across the water but the best part of a kilometre on foot.

"Go round to the clock tower," Andreas tells us. "Carry on past the shipyard and I'll be waiting by the large cactus plant." And then he sets to the task of loading and balancing our bags onto his moped.

It takes us at least half an hour to walk around the waterside to our rendezvous with Andreas. Gialos is just beginning its evening shift. Tourists in their dozens are pounding the cobbles and perusing the menus outside the tavernas. Bars and cafés are doing a brisk pre-dinner trade. We thread our way through the crowds until we reach the clock tower, actually the free-standing bell tower of the nearby Agios Ioannis church, then take a ninety-degree turn towards what Andreas described as "the shipyard." – a few wooden fishing boats and pleasure craft in various states of disrepair on a shingle beach serving as a reminder of Symi's past – until we find him. He's seated astride his moped, playing a game on his smartphone. "I waste too much time on this," he says. Thankfully, he's already deposited our bags in the studio.

We follow Andreas up a steep flight of about twenty typically Greek stone steps, uneven in both height and width, until we reach a narrow alley. No more than ten metres along the alley Andreas turns to his left and leads us up a second flight, steeper and more irregular than the first, which thankfully leads to the door of our accommodation. It's a smallish room with a balcony overlooking the harbour, a small shower room and a kitchenette. And in one corner more stairs – an almost vertical short wooden flight leading to the mezzanine bedroom, the final stage of the stairway to heaven! If nothing else, the climb from sea level to our bedroom will keep us fit.

At dinner at a harbour-side taverna called Kantirini we enjoy some basic but excellent Greek food and treat ourselves to a litre of the house red wine. And when the waiter brings our bill it's accompanied by two complimentary large glasses – of chilled red wine. It's a struggle to finish them, but we do our best.

*

It's a beautiful sunny morning and as I sit on our balcony gazing across the harbour, watching fishing boats and large yachts cruising across the millpond-flat harbour waters, I get a clue to Symi's proud past. Down to my right is the area Andreas had called the "shipyard". This little island was once home to over twenty thousand souls and built over five hundred ships and boats a year. It was said to have been where Jason's *Argo* was built and was mentioned in Homer's *Iliad* as having sent a fleet to assist in the siege of Troy. The population is now only a tenth of that, and the only hint of any maritime building is about eight beached fishing boats and cabin cruisers and the remains of a slipway into the sea. The vessels are in varying states of seaworthiness, from little more than a shell to simply needing a fresh coat of paint – but no one seems to be working on any of them. Across the road from the beach there's a workshop where a single elderly man appears to be doing something to a small dinghy, but as a shipyard it's a long way away from Harland and Wolff.

On the harbourside there's a reminder of the other industry that made Symi one of the most prosperous islands in the eastern

Mediterranean, sponge-diving. There's a life-size bronze statue of a man who looks like Gandhi but who is, according to a brass plaque on the plinth, "Stathis Hatzis, legendary naked diver". But the statue isn't there to celebrate his prolific career as a sponge-diver but an incredible feat of endurance in 1913. Over a period of three days he made a total of sixteen free dives to depths of between fifty and eighty-eight metres, holding his breath for up to four minutes at a time in an attempt to locate and secure the anchor of an Italian battleship which had been lost on the ocean floor. An exploit that makes you breathless just thinking about it.

Today it's tourism that keeps Symi prosperous, and Gialos is busy with colour-wrist-banded day-trippers from Rhodes. They stay with us until late afternoon, then pile back onto their excursion boats and leave. As we're making our way back to Marina Studios we stop and browse the menu outside a taverna near the "shipyard".

"We're fully booked this evening," says a waiter who has come out onto the street. "It's a holiday, a holiday all week in Turkey."

You can see the Turkish coast from here and the Turks do apparently love the Dodecanese. And when you look closely you realise that almost all of the yachts in the harbour are flying Turkish flags. So when we go out for dinner we go in the opposite direction, away from the main town and along the Harani seafront to the highly-recommended Tholos restaurant in the hope that things will be a little quieter. Not so. A waiter standing by the entrance shows a total lack of interest in our business.

"We're fully booked," he says in an echo of the guy we spoke to earlier but considerably less friendly. "If you don't have a reservation you can't eat here."

Fifty metres back towards Gialos is a taverna called Odyssia, where if there isn't a table obviously available they'll find you one. The staff seem to spend the entire evening shuffling tables and chairs around to cater for parties of different sizes that turn up without having booked and they turn no one away. At forty-one euros it's not the cheapest meal we've had in Greece but the goat in lemon sauce is delicious.

On the waterside almost immediately below Marina Studios is the Café Carnagio, where we stop for a nightcap. The owner, a large man in his forties with a permanent smile, treats us like long-lost relatives, serves tasty nibbles with our drinks, talks to us about our travels and makes a fuss when we leave. Greek hospitality the way you expect it to be.

*

It's eight o'clock on another warm bright morning and, like us, Gialos is just waking up. There's a gentle breeze that's keeping the temperature at a pleasant, bearable level and a few small fluffy white clouds on the tops of the higher hills that guard the town. Small boats chug out of the harbour. The eight o'clock bus to Pedi makes its way up the steep road across the water. The binmen are out on their noisy daily round. Joggers strive to complete their daily run before the day becomes too hot. Down at Café Carnagio the owner is hosing down his patio and preparing the tables and chairs for today's business. Life doesn't get much better, I feel.

After breakfast we wander into the town and in the narrow back streets come across a shop selling English daily newspapers. I can't resist a copy of *The Times*, even at four euros fifty, so long has it been since I had the chance to tackle the crossword, before we head for the bus stop and the midday service to Pedi. It costs us one-seventy each and the little twenty-seater is packed, but within fifteen minutes we've travelled up and over one of the hills that surround Gialos and found ourselves in what was once a small thriving fishing village but is now not much more than a yachting marina. There's a small sandy beach, at one end of which is a shop and at the other a bar and taverna. We find a shady spot, enjoy a cold beer, then drift back to the bus stop for the next bus back to Chorio.

This is the original island village, built some five hundred or so steps above Gialos, a maze of narrow cobbled streets and grand houses built in the eighteenth century for Symi's marauding sea captains. Some are dilapidated, the result of an explosion of German munitions during the Second World War, others have been lavishly restored. There's an archaeological museum that, ironically, is closed for restoration, and a handful of tavernas and cafés. We choose George and Maria's where we can sit on the terrace and enjoy spectacular views over the deep blue sea of Gialos harbour – and more excellent Greek food and friendly service.

Whether anyone has ever counted the steps back down into Gialos I doubt, but they're in flights of five or six at a time, with long flat stretches between them, and the descent is relatively easy, even in the heat of the afternoon sun. Almost before we know it, we're emerging onto the seafront among the souvenir shops and tavernas of the town itself.

When we walk back into the centre later there seem to be more Turkish yachts than ever tied up at the harbour, their owners either eating on board or in one of the more expensive restaurants opposite the moorings. We go a little further and, in the heart of the town, find O Meraklis, an old-school authentic taverna whose interior walls are lined with antique mirrors and old diving pictures. We sit out in the street among a really cosmopolitan clientele, listening to French, German and a variety of other languages we don't recognise. The bill, thirty-six euros, includes two half-litres of house rosé, the second a distinctly different colour from the first although both undoubtedly rosé.

And then we linger in the little park where, as part of the annual Gialos Festival, a concert is taking place. A handful of Greek musicians and a not very good, slightly out-of-tune choir. Everyone applauds politely after each song, although we suspect they're no more impressed than we are. But it's a little bit of Dodecanese culture so we shouldn't complain.

*

My first job this morning is to rescue the towel that has fallen from the airer on our balcony and onto a roof about four feet below, too far down to lean over and reach it. I contemplate climbing over the balcony but am reminded of my age and discouraged by Barbara and eventually find a solution in a floor mop behind the door in the shower room. With some difficulty I manage to manoeuvre the towel into a shape into which I can insert the end of the mop handle, then flick it upwards and catch it one-handed in mid-air. Barbara is suitably impressed by my achievement and suggests we go out for breakfast to celebrate.

We walk for most of a kilometre to the end of Harani Bay and the Nos Beach where we sit on the terrace of a taverna and enjoy cheese and ham toasties and chilled fresh orange juice. And muse upon the fact that we're eating ham. We've had ham sandwiches, pork gyros, pork steaks and all manner of different pork dishes on this and other visits to Greece. But where does it all come from? In over two decades of coming to this country neither of us can remember ever having seen a pig. On the more populous parts of the mainland there may have been the occasional smallholding where they possibly kept the odd porker or two, but not on the islands, where a lunchtime pita gyros filled with succulent pork is almost compulsory.

Refreshed and raring to face the rest of the day, we decide to walk to one of Symi's much-vaunted beaches, Nimborio. It seems like another of those 'mad dogs and Englishmen' moments, given that even around eleven o'clock it's probably thirty degrees and there won't be any shade, but it is supposed to be only four kilometres from the centre of Gialos and we're a good kilometre along the road already. It takes about three-quarters of an hour of steady walking, up and down some very gentle inclines, and we're rewarded with a fine little shingle beach with sunbeds and large umbrellas at three euros each.

A day spent reading, dozing and having lunch at the excellent Metapontis taverna is only slightly marred by two over-loud English couples a row in front of us swapping Greek holiday stories and a real brat of a small Greek child who howls every time he's rebuked by his parents or grandparents for his dreadful behaviour. Like throwing his sister's flip-flops off the jetty into the sea or hurling stones at other children on the beach or refusing to get off his grandfather's sunbed after the old man has just been to the café to buy ice creams for all the family. The Symi Taxi Boat that takes us back to Gialos harbour is empty, apart from ourselves and the man and woman crew. We sit on the front, like Kate Winslet and Leonardo DiCaprio on the *Titanic*, and enjoy our half-hour cruise.

The owner of the Café Carnagio is about to close when we stop for an after-dinner drink, our last on Symi, but he invites us to sit down, brings our drinks and, for a while, sits down beside us to talk. We tell him we're leaving tomorrow, heading for Kalymnos, but we've loved his island.

"You will come back," he says, in a tone that's somewhere between a question, a statement of fact and an order.

"We will," I tell him. "Probably not on this trip but sometime in the future." And we probably will.

CHAPTER TWO

Kalymnos – "If you don't want a receipt, I don't want the tax"

The *Dodekanisos Express*, on which we have booked tickets for Kalymnos, leaves Gialos at nine-thirty and we've arranged for Andreas to pick up our bags an hour before that. The fast Dodecanese Seaways ferries that run around the islands from Rhodes and back leave from the Harani side of the harbour, but we still don't fancy trying to manoeuvre our bags down the stairway to heaven. It's been enough of a challenge with a few groceries. Andreas is young and healthy and takes both bags down together, and we watch as he loads them onto his moped and deposits them at the base of the clock tower a couple of minutes later. We follow on, pick up the bags and settle down in a harbour-front café to enjoy a coffee.

The ferry leaves more or less on time, its wide-bodied airliner-style passenger accommodation about half-full. It's a smooth, trouble-free journey, hugging the Turkish coast for much of the way and at one point I even receive a text message from O2 welcoming me to Turkey. We spend much of the trip trying to work out what the notice on the back of the seat in front means. "Please don't throw litter at the front seat's case", it says. Has someone been bombarding the luggage of the people on the front row with rolled-up balls of paper, so frequently that a warning notice is necessary? Eventually we realise – don't leave litter in the pocket on the back of the seat in front. The rest of the time we spend watching the promotional videos for the Dodecanese showing on several TV screens around the lounge.

It's close to midday when we disembark at Pothia, the main town on Kalymnos, and we can see the accommodation Barbara has booked, the Hotel Archontiko, in front of us, no more than five minutes' walk away. We walk past the tourist information office, on the side of which is a large poster that welcomes us to "Kalymnos – the spongers' island". This presumably refers not to the large number of islanders claiming benefits but to the fact that this is the sponge-diving capital of Greece. It has the country's last sponge-diving fleet, employing four hundred people, and boats go off after Easter every year for four-month diving tours in the Aegean and around Crete. The week before is known as Sponge Week, dedicated to giving the divers a hearty send-off with plenty of food, free drinks and traditional dancing, and the eve of their departure, for obvious reasons, is called the 'Sleep of Love'.

The owner of Archontiko, Henrik, with whom Barbara's been corresponding via email, is out but a friendly Greek woman checks us in and apologises for the fact that the lift is out of order. We have to haul our bags up two flights of stairs to our room above a travel agency but it's worth it for the view when we get there. The whole of the harbour is in front of us, yachts and other pleasure craft below and to the left, ferries and other working vessels to the right, and on the opposite side of the bay, painted on an arid mountainside, is a huge Greek flag.

After we've unpacked, we take a walk along the sea front, stop for a drink at one of the many cafés and bars, then have a late lunch at Manias fish taverna. The young Australian waiter, a student working the summer on the island of his parents' birth, recommends a local speciality, delicious small fried shrimps and a Kalymnian salad, a good start to our few days on the island. This isn't a traditional seaside resort, but the quayside is lined with old mansions and statues of various sea gods and on a Sunday lunchtime, families are out in force. We even find a small supermarket on the seafront that's open. And on our return to the Archontiko we find Henrik in reception, Danish, fiftyish, gayish – no, not 'ish', very camp and someone to whom we immediately warm. He's a complete contrast to what our guidebook has warned us to expect, "rugged Kalymnians known throughout history for their toughness and terse manner." Less rugged and terse you couldn't imagine.

At Pantelis, described as a "homey taverna" a short walk from Archontiko, we're lucky to walk in and get a table straight away. It's clearly popular, arguably the most popular eating house in Pothia, since no sooner are we seated than other people begin queuing at the entrance, some eventually giving up and walking away. It's easy to understand why. This evening's 'specials', goat in lemon sauce and homemade dolmades, are excellent and the house wine is only four euros fifty a half-litre. But we're not sure we would have had the patience to wait for a table as long as some of the customers appear to be waiting, as much as an hour, it seems. Some have been getting very agitated, arguing with waiters and trying to claim tables that aren't occupied but have been reserved. The staff have a difficult job, but do their best to keep everyone happy, and are worth the generous tip we leave them.

*

Despite our position in the heart of the town it's been a quiet night, but our room faces east and we're woken early by the bright sun streaming in at the floor-to-ceiling window. That and the bells – we're almost next-door to Pothia's main church – mean that we don't get much of a lie-in. Since Henrik doesn't provide cooking facilities other than a kettle, we have breakfast out, delicious omelettes at the Miami café on the quayside. We buy some groceries from the well-stocked Synka supermarket, take them back to our room at the Archontiko and head for the bus terminal to take the noon service to the west of the island and the little beach resort of Myrties.

The bus is packed, with standing room only after the first couple of stops, and passengers are forced to sit next to, and talk to, complete strangers. A man and a woman, both aged about sixty, sitting across the aisle from us strike up a conversation. They talk in Greek for a few minutes before they realise that Greek is not their first language and they switch to English. Heavily Australian-accented English. They are both from Melbourne, which has the largest number of Greek-speakers anywhere, other than Athens, and are paying the regular visit to the 'rellies' back in the homeland. The more they talk, the more they have in common. They know the same areas of Melbourne, they even have some mutual acquaintances. Given the number of Greeks who moved to Australia in the diaspora of the fifties and sixties and who come back fairly frequently, it's probably not that uncommon, but it's fascinating anyway.

Myrties is slightly disappointing, and other than the water taxi to the little island of Telendos, which we intend to visit later, there isn't a great deal to do or see. There's a small beach with no shade and no umbrellas, a couple of tavernas and not much else. We walk along the road for a couple of hundred metres, and sit down at the Ethereal bar, organic and slightly pretentious but surprising in that our two beers come to only seven euros sixty, and then return to the beach area and have lunch at Stalas. We watch the little boats going backwards and forwards between Myrties and Telendos while enjoying shrimp saganaki and a tuna salad, washed down with a half-litre of house white, then head for some shade by the roadside to await the bus back to Pothia.

It's not the only time I enjoy shrimp saganaki today. This evening we go to the highly recommended Barba Yannis on the Pothia quayside, described by our guidebook as a "great spot for traditional Greek dishes". I've actually ordered mussels but for some reason I get the shrimps in fried cheese again. But it *is* good, so I don't complain.

Back at the Archontiko we sit on our balcony with a Metaxa nightcap and watch the *Nissos Chios* steam into the port, the biggest vessel we've seen in Pothia so far and presumably on the same run as the one that took us into Symi last week. There's a huge amount of activity around the quayside, taxis coming and going, backpackers striding along the seafront, and a few minutes after the ship's arrival there's the sound downstairs of Henrik welcoming new guests to the hotel. And then, while the *Nissos Chios* is still docked, a second ferry arrives, Anek Seas Lines. Such excitement, and we have a grandstand view. Will life ever be the same again?

*

This morning I finished reading *Winds of Crete*, a little book a friend gave to me a few weeks ago after finding it in a charity shop. It was written by an American, David MacNeill Doren, in the mid-1970s about the years he lived on the island with his Swedish wife during the sixties, a strange, old-fashioned writing style but interesting, nonetheless. Today, we decide, should be a day for taking life easy, for exploring what it the third-largest town in the Dodecanese on foot. It's a labyrinth of narrow cobbled streets lined with attractive mansions and high-walled gardens. It's lively and noisy and makes no concessions to the tourist trade.

We spend time following signs directing us to the "Museum", the Archaeological Museum which we've read is housed in a neo-classical mansion once owned by the Vouvalis family, the first merchants to export sponges from Kalymnos. We've also read that it's hidden in the back streets and hard to find. And so it proves. So hard, in fact, that we eventually give up, even though we know we can't be far away. Another day perhaps. The museum's highlight, a larger-than-life-size second-century BC bronze statue of a woman discovered in the sea off Kalymnos in 1994, *has* to be seen apparently.

On the waterfront again, we stop at Stukas taverna, a friendly little family-run establishment, where we have a leisurely late morning drink and watch the world go by. And the middle-aged woman we assume is Mama Stukas seated at the rear of the terrace, near the entrance to the kitchen, preparing the day's dolmades. Her nimble fingers flatten large vine leaves, scoop a handful of spiced mincemeat and rice from a big cast-iron pot and place it on a flattened leaf, then carefully fold the leaf and put it in a saucepan. Not only is it fascinating to watch, the dolmades are clearly delicious. As we watch, a postman on his scooter arrives at the front of the taverna with a package and he needs a signature before he can hand it over. Mama Stukas disappears into the kitchen to find a pen and while she's away the postman dips into the saucepan four or five times, polishing off the uncooked dolmades with obvious relish.

We have our own delicious lunch, pita gyros and a beer, outside a fast-food café on a corner near our hotel, and watch the wrist-banded day-trippers wandering up and down the waterfront and wondering where they are and why they're here.

Half a dozen boatloads come into the harbour every day from Kos, boats built to look like pirate ships with names like *Captain Hook* or *Black Pearl*. They spend between two and five hours here as part of an 'island-hopping' excursion for which they pay at least fifty euros. Watching them walk past our table in groups of anything from two to twenty, then walk back the other way five minutes later, makes us feel slightly superior.

This evening we make our second visit of the day to Stukas taverna. Mama Stukas, or Mama Popi as she's described on the menu, is in the kitchen, still cooking almost twelve hours after we first saw her preparing the dolmades. It's one of the friendliest Greek restaurants we've ever encountered. We get a free appetiser as well as a small pudding, the swordfish (fried on the recommendation of the waiter) is excellent, as are Barbara's "spair ribs" (*sic*), and with a litre of house red wine the bill is less than thirty-five euros.

Henrik is still in the reception area when we get back to Archontiko, waiting for the arrival of more guests on the late ferry. He seems genuinely pleased to see us and asks how we're enjoying Kalymnos. Enormously, we tell him before asking how a Dane found himself running a hotel on a small Greek island.

"I'd had twenty-five years as a flight attendant," he replies, waving his left hand in a gesture that suggests it was decades ago. "It was time for something different. I had some friends who were living here and they said I should try it so I came for a visit and bought a plot of land to build a house. Then I found this place. It's eight years now and I absolutely love it."

"You speak Greek now?"

He smiles. "After a fashion. I've had classes and learned enough to get by. Then I met an English lady who's also moved here. She comes to the hotel once a week and we spend the afternoon together, drinking tea and speaking only Greek to each other. It's great fun."

"And will you stay here?" I ask. "Do you miss Denmark at all?"

"What do you think?" he answers. "Maybe when I'm too old to look after myself I'll go back and live with my nephew or niece. But you know, you obviously love Greece as well. I travelled all over the world when I was with the airline, but at the moment I can't think of anything I'd rather do than be here."

*

It's dull and cloudy, not what the forecast yesterday evening had suggested it may be, but as the morning goes on the sun makes a serious attempt to burn off the cloud. We plan to get the eleven o'clock bus to Myrties again and take the water taxi over to Telendos. But at the bus station by the port we're told by a man in the kiosk that there's no service to that side of the island today.

"The bus is broken," he tells us. "We're waiting for a technician."

Fifteen minutes later, as we sit outside a café with a cup of strong coffee wondering what to do, we see him emerge from the kiosk with a handful of A4 sheets of paper and a roll of Sellotape. He tapes one of the sheets on the window of the kiosk, then jumps onto a quad bike and heads off into the town, presumably to tape notices announcing the cancellation of today's services on bus stops along the route.

We have a brainwave. We'll go back to Archontiko and seek Henrik's advice about what to do. We've wanted to go to Telendos, even if it's just another island-grab, so maybe we can get a taxi.

"Too expensive," says Henrik when we tell him our thoughts. "Maybe fifteen or twenty euros each way. The water taxi's not cheap either. And there's not much to see at Telendos. It's a pretty little island but there's nothing there. No, if you can, you should take the bus to Vlychadia. It's a lovely beach and there's a really good taverna called Paradisio right on the beach."

What he hasn't said is that the bus is free, possibly because of its age. It's an ancient twenty-five-seat boneshaker that struggles to climb hills then careers down the other side as if it's out of control. It brings back memories of Folegrandros.

"It's a collector's item, this," an elderly Greek man, the only other passenger when we leave the bus station, says sardonically. "It's from another era."

The bus makes random stops to pick up and set down as it crosses some wonderfully barren country over one of the highest points of the island and deposits us at Vlychadia twenty-five minutes after leaving. This is a real gem, not mentioned in any guidebook we've looked at, and we're grateful to Henrik and the fact that the Myrties bus had broken down. There are two small beaches, one sandy and one pebbles, and about four tavernas. We settle down at Paradisio and enjoy our first little fish for some time – it's been 'out of season' for weeks – and a really good local salad.

In one of the side roads leading away from the beach we find a tiny minimarket with a small garden to one side where is seated a man of about seventy, reading a thick hardback book.

"Do you have ice cream?" we ask, then feel rather foolish as we spot the large chest fridge whirring away a few feet from where he's sitting. He makes a gesture that we take to mean 'help yourselves' and we open the lid. Inside there are about a dozen unlabelled tubs. "Made from local milk," the man says. They cost two euros each and are exquisite.

He then pulls two chairs from under the table at which he's sitting and asks us to join him.

"What country are you from?" he asks. "America?" We tell him we're English. "Where from?" he continues. "North, south, middle?"

"From the south coast," I reply. "From Brighton."

"Brighton," he says, his face lighting up. "My son was at university in Brighton. He was at Guildford for four years and then he did a Masters degree in Brighton." I silently wonder if he knew our landlord in Kythira. "In satellite communications. Now he works in Oxford and he comes home every summer for a holiday."

"Do you go over to England to visit him?"

He shakes his head. "Not anymore. My wife and my other sons go but I don't. I used to be a seaman. I went all over the world when I was younger. Now I just stay here, where I was born. I'm happy."

We thank him for the ice cream, he shakes our hands vigorously and wishes us luck, and we head back towards the bus stop and the free theme park ride back to Pothia.

There's a buzz on the Pothia waterfront later that evening as men settle down outside cafés to watch football on large TV screens. Local favourites PAOK are playing Benfica in a qualifying round of the Champions League and we join the excited crowd at a bar called Déjà Vu. It starts well and PAOK take the lead after less than ten minutes. But by the time we leave it's four-one to the Portuguese team and subdued doesn't really do the atmosphere justice.

*

Will the bus to Myrties be running today, we wonder, as we make our way towards the bus station in a temperature that has already reached thirty-five degrees by midday. The answer, we soon discover, is no. "Maybe at one o'clock," the woman at the bus station tells us, but it's a big fat Greek maybe. We seek out the post office in Pothia's back streets and despatch some postcards, have a drink outside a café that has a view across the harbour to the bus station – just in case the bus dramatically appears – then take the free two o'clock boneshaker, this time to Vathy about fifteen kilometres away on the other side of the island and alleged to be very pretty.

And so it proves. We have an impressive journey along some stunning coastal scenery and across barren hills populated only by goats until we descend to sea level at Rina, the pretty little harbour hamlet adjoining Vathy. We settle down outside Poppy's taverna where a small middle-aged woman we assume to be Poppy herself suggests we might like to try the pastitsio. Whether there's anything else on the menu, apart from the ubiquitous Greek salad, we don't bother asking. Poppy doesn't look like the sort of woman you'd want to start an argument with. And the pastitsio *is* very good.

We spend a couple of lazy hours relaxing on the beach and reading until, shortly before we're due to get the bus back to Pothia, we and the rest of the people enjoying the afternoon are entertained by the crew of a large yacht called *Caitlin*. It's registered in Glasgow and from their loud conversation the crew of what appears to be four couples are undoubtedly British. But whether any of them has had any previous sailing experience we very much doubt as we watch them try to manoeuvre the yacht into the little marina. They reverse in and out at least half a dozen times. They throw ropes out of the boat, then haul them in again. They attempt to tie up at at least three different berths. The process continues for a full half an hour as the fifty or so people at the beach watch in silence, and we're still not sure whether or not they've cracked it by the time we have to go back up the road and get the boneshaker to Pothia.

There's a totally different atmosphere around the bars and cafés of Pothia this evening. It's Olympiacos's turn to try and win a Europa League qualifier, they have a three-one lead over Burnley from the first leg and when we leave the Déjà Vu after our nightcap it's well into the second half and that lead is still intact. Happy days are clearly here again.

Back at Archontiko Henrik is in reception and since this is our last night on the island, we decide to pay him.

"Do you want the tourist tax?" I ask after we've counted out a wad of twenty-euro notes.

"Do you want a receipt?" Henrik replies. We don't and he doesn't. He's clearly immersed himself completely in the Greek way of life.

CHAPTER THREE

Lipsi – "They've been coming here even longer than we have"

Packed and ready to leave Kalymnos, we have another excellent breakfast omelette at the Miami café, pick up our bags from reception, bid our farewells to Henrik and walk round to the port. As the *Dodekanisos Express* nears the quay we notice a group of about twenty women of all ages, all dressed in black and accompanied by a priest. We speculate on where they may be going. Some kind of pilgrimage, perhaps? We hadn't noticed the silver-grey hearse until a van that had been obscuring our view moves off. The ferry docks, and as the rear ramp is lowered some of the women begin wailing and crossing themselves furiously. Once the ramp is fully down, six men carry a coffin off the ferry and place it in the back of the hearse, which then slowly drives away in the direction of the town, followed by the priest and his entourage of mourning women. Is it someone who's lived and died in another part of Greece and is being brought home? Has someone suffered an illness or had an accident while travelling? We're about to leave Kalymnos so we'll probably never know.

The ferry is busy and running late but after a journey of ninety minutes arrives in the port on the little island of Lipsi, on what is now a searingly hot afternoon. 'Little' being the operative word, it's no more than eight kilometres from end to end and most of its seven hundred inhabitants live here in the only village. It's a dramatic sight, the village spread around the edge of a large natural harbour and up the small hill that surrounds it, dominated by the blue-domed church of St John. It was here, according to Homer, that Odysseus was seduced by the charms of the nymph Calypso and delayed his return home for seven years. He had Penelope waiting for him back on Ithaca, but, stepping onto the quayside from the ferry, it's not difficult to understand why he was reluctant to leave.

We've booked accommodation in the village at Katerina Studios and been told by email that no one will be available to meet us off the ferry. There isn't a taxi in sight, so we show a piece of paper on which the address is written to an elderly woman on the quay. She says something in Greek and points to a street about three hundred metres away that runs into the village proper. We pull our bags around the water's edge, then take the turning indicated and a couple of blocks back spot a large sign reading 'Katerina' on the roof of one of the whitewashed concrete blocks. On the first-floor communal balcony we're welcomed by a tall Greek woman of about forty who we assume to be Katerina herself and who welcomes us warmly and apologises that our room isn't ready.

"Ten minutes," she says, inviting us to sit at one of the tables on the balcony and bringing us glasses of iced water. Three-quarters of an hour and a great deal of activity with brooms, vacuum cleaners and linen later we're allowed into a nicely furnished apartment with a good-sized private balcony overlooking the garden. It's quiet, a complete contrast to Kalymnos, and from the balcony I can count eleven churches of different sizes and one small field containing three sheep.

This evening, quite by chance, we stumble across Manolis Tastes, in the heart of the village and with the reputation of being the best restaurant on the island. It's in an attractive nineteenth-century building that served as the police station under the Italian occupation and Manolis himself is apparently recognised as far away as Athens for his culinary skill and imagination. It's busy but they manage to find a table for us, and while the food is very good we're at something of a loss to understand why it's quite so highly regarded. One thing we are certain of, however, is the size of the portions, which in the main are far too large to finish. We're not the only diners requesting a doggy bag.

*

It's been a hot night and at some time midway through it we took the decision to use the air-conditioning. Not a decision taken lightly because for one thing we don't like the noise and for another we're uneasy about the effects of air-con on the environment. But when you wake in the middle of the night bathed in sweat it seems like the only option if you're to get a decent remainder-of-the-night's sleep. At nine o'clock it's almost unbelievably quiet. The bells of some of the eleven churches we can see from the balcony are ringing. Two cockerels are trying to out-crow each other. A dog is barking. Goats' bells are ringing their dull tinny ring. An old motor-scooter splutters up the narrow lane to our right. It's all surprisingly peaceful.

We take the little municipal bus to Katsadia beach, a couple of kilometres south of Lipsi village. We're the only people on board, apart from the driver, a friendly bearded local man, and it costs us a euro each for an enjoyable ten-minute journey. We could have walked but by the time we're ready to go it's much too hot. Katsadia is a truly beautiful spot, a narrow unspoiled sandy beach and a single taverna offering shade and shelter from the wind. We linger over a very good lunch, our attention grabbed at one point by a snake that slithers across the stone floor from one shaded spot to another. It's a small skinny thing about eighteen inches long and nowhere near as chunky as the monster that scared us on Iraklia, but it's still enough to cause Barbara, and a number of other diners, to lift her feet off the floor.

Back at Katerina Studios in the late afternoon there's no electricity. It's been off since about one o'clock apparently. A German couple staying in one of the other studios are seated on the communal balcony and they tell us, "It's normal here," but assure us that something is being done to fix it. They're right, and by five power is restored.

*

Early yesterday evening there were hints that a wedding was taking place somewhere in the village. Church bells were chiming sporadically, a good deal of shouting could be heard, as well as what we believed was the occasional firing of shotguns. But when we went out for dinner, we didn't see any sign of it. But my, did we hear the party during the night – all night. It went on until at least eight o'clock this morning, music in the not-too-far distance, explosions of either gunfire or fireworks, shouts and screams of people obviously enjoying themselves. A real Greek wedding and we should have expected it. Our guidebook warns that when there's a wedding on Lipsi "the whole island celebrates with a joyous all-night dance marathon".

As a result, we don't get going too early this morning, but when we do we take the midday municipal minibus to Platis Gialos, three kilometres over the backbone of the island. It's the island's best-known beach, a small semi-circular cove sloping gently into the sea. Unlike yesterday, when we were the only passengers going to Katsadia, the bus is busy – as is the beach when we get there. It's narrow and probably no more than a hundred metres from end to end but it's fringed with trees that offer welcome shade from the early afternoon sun. It's a popular spot for families, particularly one that takes up about half the space in the only taverna, ensuring that service is slow for everyone else.

There must be at least twenty of them from all generations, speaking loudly in a mixture of American- and Australian-accented English and Greek. They're spread along both sides of a long table and we're seated next to them. Despite the noise they're making, it isn't long before one of them, a middle-aged man, recognises that we're speaking English and approaches us to apologise for the noise – and for monopolising the staff who are delivering mountains of food to their table. We don't mind, we tell him, and, by the way, from your accent you clearly don't live on Lipsi.

"I was born here," he says. "But I went to live in California twenty-five years ago." He goes on to explain that he has two sisters, one of whom lives in Australia and one who still lives on the island. They're both here, along with their husbands and children, as well as his own wife and sons, their parents and some of their in-laws. It's the first time all the family has been together for at least fifteen years, and for some of the children it's the first time they've been to Lipsi. They've taken over most of one of the hotels in the village, he says, and if we're around one evening he'll buy us a drink and we can talk some more.

*

Our cooking facilities in Katerina Studios are, to say the least, a little eccentric. We have a three-ring hob, which is something of a luxury, being fifty per cent bigger than most Greek holiday hobs, *and* a small oven. The trouble is, you can't use both at the same time. If you want a boiled egg with soldiers, say, you first have to boil the eggs on one of the hobs, then switch it off, and turn on the grill part of the oven to make the toast – which makes preparing breakfast a pretty drawn-out affair. We reported it to Katerina who came and examined the facilities, shrugged her shoulders in a way that said, "What's wrong with that?" and left us to it. It's quite late when we get up this morning, and we don't want to spoil our lunch, so we settle for just toast.

We have a lazy day doing little other than sitting alternately in the sun and the shade, eating, drinking and reading, until we go out for dinner this evening. Taverna Yannis is at the far end of the waterfront near the ferry terminal and has an excellent balcony from which to people-watch. Down on the pavement below us they've laid out a long table which a quick count shows is ready to seat forty-eight. We're grateful we came out when we did. Being after four dozen other diners could mean an awfully long wait for food. We assume it's the Lipsi-American-Australian family we met yesterday, but when they arrive it's a party of people who are all probably in their thirties and forties and speaking in a European language we don't recognise.

What we do recognise is the English being spoken by the two couples on the table nearest to us, Britons trying to outscore each other with their best and worst Greek holiday experiences. They've probably only met in the last day or two and all four believe that they 'discovered' Lipsi. Until, that is, one of the women remembers a conversation she had with a Swedish couple a few days ago. "Nice people," she says patronisingly. "And they've been coming here *even longer* than *we* have."

*

We're up early this morning for an island grab. Leros will be the forty-first island we've either visited or stayed on in two decades of travelling to Greece. Our return tickets on the *Patmos Star*, the little ferry service that runs between the islands in this part of the Dodecanese, have cost thirty-four euros (eight euros fifty each way) but in the interests of seeing another Greek island it's worth it.

It's busy down at the port and the *Patmos Star* is, almost inevitably, twenty minutes late. It's a smooth comfortable crossing – although not for one small boy of about eight or nine travelling with his grandparents. He complains of feeling sick and is instantly grabbed by the collar of his shirt and dragged to the nearest litter bin by his grandmother. She thrusts his head into the bin until he's well enough, although still distinctly pale, to sit down again.

Leros once had an unenviable reputation as the home of one of Greece's most notorious mental hospitals and was even exposed in a British TV documentary thirty years ago. Nowadays, it's a pretty, welcoming island, popular with holidaymakers who just want to unwind on their favourite beach. It's also said to have been the original home of the goddess of the hunt, Artemis, and the little port village of Agia Marina, where we're deposited by the *Patmos Star*, is overlooked by the ancient ruined fortress of Pandelis. The oldest parts of the castle date back more than a millennium, but outer ramparts were added in the fourteenth and fifteenth centuries. There isn't a great deal left, but it's worth the walk up the steep stepped path to enjoy the breathtaking all-round views.

Back down in Agia Marina we wander along the waterfront, browsing the souvenir shops before enjoying a pre-lunch drink and settling down at a port-side taverna called Ta Kroupia for excellent pita gyros and a Greek salad. A couple of tables away are the grandparents from the ferry and their grandson, who is being force-fed chips although he's clearly still unwell. We can't help feeling sorry for the boy. It's almost the end of the school holidays and a day trip to Leros with Yiayia and Papou was no doubt meant as a treat.

*

Pilgrims from the surrounding islands apparently descend on Lipsi in their hundreds in August for the "ninth day of the Virgin", a modern miracle in which dead flowers are reborn. In the Panagia tou Charou, a little church outside the main village, there's an icon, and the story goes that a poor woman once prayed there to the Virgin to help her sick son and her prayers were answered. She had nothing with which to repay the Virgin apart from a lily, which she placed by the icon. The lily withered, of course, but on the day of the Virgin's acceptance into Heaven it sprang into full bloom, and it has flowered on that day ever since. The lily's rootless and unwatered stalk can still be seen behind the glass of the icon and at this time of year it should be surrounded by other dried and apparently dead flowers which have allegedly burst into life on 24th August.

It's probably no more than a couple of kilometres from our accommodation to the church, but in this heat even a two-kilometre walk can be an ordeal. We set off before nine and it takes us about half an hour, up the road that takes us out of the village then down into the valley where we can see the church on the way to one of the beaches. It's a hot, quiet morning and all we can see and hear is farm animals – goats, sheep, chickens, even a few cattle (but no pigs!) – but when we reach the church it appears that we're going to be disappointed. Despite a printed notice announcing that it is open from 09.00–13.00, the door is firmly locked.

Somewhat disconsolately, we wander around the outside of the church, taking photographs and bemoaning our ill luck. We think for one moment that we may perhaps have come to the wrong place, but across the road on what is normally used as a car park, a small, rather flimsy grandstand has been erected and on the side of the church facing it are several loudspeakers. Clearly something important happens here at some time. And then, as we're about to leave, we hear the sound of an approaching moped and a middle-aged woman arrives at the church and unlocks the door. Surprisingly, there's an elderly woman already inside the building. Is she locked in all night, we wonder, a kind of geriatric security guard? They exchange a few words before the younger woman gets back on her moped and rides off.

While we look around the pretty little church the old woman busies herself polishing and tidying things. On a central pillar the icon which is said to be unique is a portrait of the Virgin Mary cradling the crucified Christ. It's behind a glass screen with what we assume are several unwatered lilies at each side. If they had burst into life it was a few weeks ago and they've withered again. The little tableau is surrounded by dozens of cheap tin votives depicting arms, legs, hearts, babies, even houses, placed there by grateful pilgrims. It must be quite a sight on the day the lilies bloom. We thank the old woman, shove a five-euro note in the church's collection box and head back to the village.

There's supposed to be at least one other interesting location on the island. At least that's what the map of the island we've managed to acquire indicates. Just past the village's own beach, Liendou – a couple of minutes' walk over a small headland – is Campos, an archaeological site according to the map. After a late breakfast involving some delicious bread that we've bought at our neighbourhood bakery we go in search of it. What we find is a scrubby fenced-off area about the size of a tennis court. No signage, no obvious signs of ancient ruins. We're not even sure it's the right place. But it's getting hot now and we can't be bothered searching any more.

*

One of the more surprising things about Lipsi, or at least the main village, is how busy it can become in the evening. Nowhere else to go, presumably, the tavernas on the beaches all closing in the late afternoon. Manolis Tastes, the first place we come to as we walk into the village, is packed and can only offer us a table out in the street. We turn down their offer and instead settle down outside the Café du Moulin in the little square beside the church of St John. It serves good inexpensive food and we're given a free ouzo at the end of our meal. But more interesting than the meal is the fact that the elderly woman who appears to run the taverna and several other seventy-something locals are seated outside the kitchen conversing in heavily accented French. I nod towards them when the waitress brings our bill. "Why are they speaking French?"

She smiles. "They're Belgian," she answers in flawless English. "The owner and her husband came here in the nineteen-sixties for a holiday and stayed. I don't think they've ever been back to Belgium, or to any other island. Then other members of the family joined them. They all speak Greek very well of course, but they love to get together and speak French. I'm lucky, I studied French at university so I can understand them, but no one else here can."

Down in the town park, the mystery of the forty-odd people who were at Yannis the other evening speaking a language we didn't understand is solved. They're a Finnish folk dance and music troupe giving one of a series of concerts around the islands during the summer. We watch for a while, a curious colourful mix of Morris dancing and Scandi singing being appreciated by an audience that's somewhat smaller than the size of the troupe, before heading to an ouzerie on the harbour for a last drink or two on Lipsi. We haven't bumped into the Greek-Australian-American family we met at the beach three or four days ago but now we find ourselves next to a similar group. There's about twenty of them, speaking a mixture of Greek and Australian-accented English and they're celebrating two birthdays – one of an elderly woman, the grandmother of many of the group, the other a young woman who, various clues tell us, is twenty-five today. It's another warm friendly family group that wishes us well on our travels around their islands. We love Lipsi as much as these people clearly do and we'll be a little sad to move on.

Chapter Four

Patmos – "A beast rose up out of the sea"

A young man we assume to be a member of Katerina's family has been to see us, knocking quietly on the door of our studio and politely asking if everything about our stay has been in order. Very much so, we tell him, and pay him in cash, as requested, a sum that equates to little more than thirty euros a night. A few minutes later he returns with a gift, a small bar of beautifully perfumed soap in a Katerina Studios wrapper, and is kind enough to carry the heavier of our two bags down to the street. Down at the port it's busy, not least because the forty-odd Finnish folk singers and dancers are waiting for the same ferry, posing for group photographs and bidding farewell to their Lipsi hosts.

The little island of Patmos, our next destination, punches way above its weight. Barely a dot on most maps, it is known as the "holy island", or sometimes the "island of the Apocalypse", and to the majority of Greek Christians it is the most sacred of all the country's islands. Here St John the Theologian, or John the Divine, or the Evangelist, lived in exile almost two thousand years ago and received the vision of the end of the world that he described in the New Testament Book of Revelation. You take these things with a pinch of salt, of course, but apart from the dramatic beauty of an island that is less than ten kilometres from top to bottom and only a few metres wide at its waist, it's definitely St John that draws you here.

According to the scriptures, St John came to Patmos in the first century AD, banished by the Roman emperor Domitian, and lived in a cave above what is now the main village of Skala. Here he is said to have heard the voice of God coming from a cleft in a rock, and in the Book of Revelation wrote "And I stood upon the sand of the sea and saw a beast rise up out of the sea, having seven heads and ten horns." And with that, according to some sources, he left, returning to Ephesus on the mainland of what is now Turkey after little more than a year on the island but having had sufficient time to foresee the fall of the Roman Empire.

Patmos was abandoned in the seventh century, regarded as a barren rock not worth defending. But four hundred years later the Byzantine emperor of the day gave a saintly hermit called Christodoulos permission, and the funds, to build a monastery in St John's memory, a monastery that became a fortress against the frequent pirate raids, and Patmos began to flourish again. It's that monastery, and the cave in which St John received his vision, that we're planning to see today.

We arrive at the bus station on the harbour at Skala to see one bus disappearing into the distance and to discover that the next one isn't due for another ninety minutes. On a blazing hot morning the thought of walking is more than we can take. A taxi driver loitering nearby says he will take us there for eight euros. He'll even wait and bring us back down to Skala if we wish. It takes him only five minutes to whisk us up to Chora, where we make a note of his phone number and tell him we'll call him if we need a ride back down. We linger to enjoy the incredible views of the island then make our way up through the narrow cobbled, whitewashed-house-lined alleys to the Monastery of St John the Theologian.

Running the gauntlet of tacky souvenir sellers around the entrance, we pay our four-euro entry fees and find ourselves in a courtyard, the highlight of which is the impressively frescoed twelfth-century Chapel of the Theotokos. Despite its size, this is a working monastery, only a small part of which is open to visitors. But that includes the Treasury Museum where the original monastery deed signed by the emperor in 1088 is on display, alongside gold and silver crosses, crosiers and stoles, wonderful icons, ship pendants decorated with diamonds and emeralds given to the monastery by Catherine the Great and an original El Greco painting.

We'd been warned to get here early to beat the cruise ship passengers and we're glad we did. It gets busier as the morning goes on but we manage to stay one step ahead. It's a short walk down to the Monastery of the Apocalypse which, because it's so poorly signposted, we almost miss. It's built around the cave where St John lived as a hermit and dreamed his revelation. The cave has been converted into a little church that's already busy with believers being given an organised tour by a solemn-looking priest. We sit on one of the low narrow benches and listen, Barbara managing to pick up some of what the man is saying.

In one corner of the cave is a recess in the wall where St John is reputed to have rested his head when he slept, a stone slab said to have been his writing desk and a handhold which he is supposed to have used to haul himself up from his prayers. Like most of us, his knees clearly gave way before the rest of his body if he needed help to haul himself up, although he must have been something of a contortionist to have worked, slept and prayed in the way it's suggested he did. As various parts of the cave are pointed out to them, the believers cross themselves several times then kiss one or more of the many icons. It's a ritual I don't really understand, but it's a fascinating experience, nonetheless.

*

In a smart little minimarket in the back streets of Skala we're served by a Greek man of about forty.

"Are you from Great Britain?" he asks, which is unusual because the question is normally "Where are you from?" or "Are you English?"

"Whereabouts?" he continues after we confirm that we are indeed British, and when we tell him where we live he nods and says, "Nice place."

"You know it?" To most Greek men Brighton normally means a newish Premier League football team and very little else.

"I was in England for three years," he replies. "I was at university. I travelled all over the country."

Now it's our turn to ask, "Whereabouts?"

"University of Essex."

"Colchester!" Barbara almost shrieks in delight. "I was born in Colchester."

"And we got married there," I chip in, not wanting to be left out of the conversation.

"Essex girl," he says with a wry smile. "Very nice."

We spend some minutes discussing the merits of England's oldest recorded town before we gather up our purchases and leave. We can't help wondering what brought an educated man back to a tiny island in the Aegean after three years experiencing the delights of South East England but feel disinclined to ask. Mersea Island doesn't get the sunshine that Patmos does, I suppose.

*

After stumbling across a small shop in another of the pretty little cobbled alleys that sells same-day English newspapers and being able to buy my first copy of *The Times* since Symi, we're sitting outside a café on Sakla's harbour front enjoying an early evening pre-dinner drink when we become aware of a group of priests emerging from a side street. There's about seven of them in all, some of them wearing those long brightly coloured scarves that indicate they're about to conduct some kind of service, one of them chanting at a level that can barely be heard. And then, from the same side street that is only just wide enough for it to have squeezed through, a hearse appears, carrying a coffin and covered in floral tributes.

After the hearse come about two hundred people, mostly women and mostly clothed from head to toe in black. A silence seems to descend on the entire seafront area, cars come to a standstill, people sitting outside the cafés like ourselves bow their heads and cross themselves as the procession makes its way towards whatever church is hosting the service. It's a solemn, sombre occasion – or rather it would be if not for the fact that at least two of the mourners are having mobile phone conversations, no doubt describing the scene to others who can't be there, while several others are engaged in conversations that can only be described as frivolous. Exchanging happy memories of the deceased, we speculate.

Chapter Five

Kos – "Closed due to earthquake damage"

We're having to stay on Kos slightly longer than we'd planned. We booked a two-night stay in Kos town and tickets for a ferry that will take us on to Tilos fairly early in the morning on the third day. But about a week ago, not long after we'd booked it, I had a text from the Hellenic Seaways. Our old friend the *Nissos Chios* won't be leaving Kos at eight o'clock in the morning after all. It's been 'rearranged' to a quarter past one the following morning, leaving us with a full day on Kos instead of almost a full day on Tilos and meaning that we arrive on Tilos at some unearthly hour in the middle of the night. Barbara has been in touch with the accommodation we've booked there, informing them of the change in our travel arrangements, but since they're almost certainly aware of the 'rearranged' ferry schedule they're no doubt ready for it.

Kos is another of those places that's described in the guidebooks as a "resort island", a paradise for beach-lovers and a rival to Rhodes as the major tourist attraction of the Dodecanese. We're really only here because there's no other practical way of getting from Lipsi to Tilos. The *Dodekanisi Pride* takes three hours, calling at Lipsi, Leros and Kalymnos again and there's the almost predictable chaos when we dock in Kos town. We, the Finnish folk-dancers and singers and what appears to be a large party of basketball-playing schoolchildren from Patmos struggle to find the right luggage as it's hauled onto the quayside by the ferry's crew. Once we do, it takes about fifteen minutes to find the Pantheon Studios in a street a couple of blocks back from the waterfront.

The seafront area is pretty much as expected, apart from the fact that for such a smart-looking town the walkway is in serious need of repair and to walk along it is to risk stumbling over broken and upturned paving slabs. On our right, the harbour, lined with the pirate ship day-excursion boats of the type we watched coming in and out of the harbour at Kalymnos. On our left, wall-to-wall bars and cafés with names like Big Ben and Blues Brothers and advertising happy hours and live English Premier League football. Across the water, only a few kilometres away, we can see the Turkish coast and the popular resort of Bodrum, a magnet for day-trippers. But away from the front it's much more authentically Greek, although many of the picturesque little streets have been turned into shopping malls selling cheap souvenirs and over-priced tee-shirts. It's something of a culture shock after the quiet little islands we've stayed on recently.

We dump our bags in our second-floor room at the Pantheon – spacious but not quite of the standard we've become used to – and set off in search of a late lunch. Within no more than twenty metres of our front door we have Chinese, Italian and Mexican restaurants, as well as a number of tavernas, and we eventually settle for a tiny grill house called Lefteris, which seems to cater more for the takeaway trade than sit-down customers but nevertheless serves us excellent pita gyros at two euros twenty each and a half-litre of house wine for three fifty.

We hadn't realised just how spoiled for choice we are until we go out for dinner. After a short walk up and down the street we sit down outside Noah's Ark, almost directly opposite our accommodation. We're offered a free tabouleh as a starter and are then served some delicious food in generous portions before being given a shot of something warm and clearly quite strong to finish. It's a family-owned Armenian establishment and after we've finished our food, the chef-owner Aris, a short fifty-something Armenian with a permanent smile, comes out of his kitchen to talk to us. He's been in Kos for twenty-four years, he tells us, and he loves the island. Inevitably, he asks where we're from and seems overjoyed when we tell him.

"Ah England," he says, beaming. "I love the English people very much. Especially the Welsh and the Scotch!"

*

This is a very different place from anywhere we've been recently. There's a real exciting buzz about Kos town, but although it's noisy – with constant traffic, loud cicadas, the clatter of plates and cutlery in the restaurant kitchens and a band playing in a taverna just across the street – we've slept well. We've only planned to do one thing on the island, although our enforced prolonged stay tomorrow will give us time for more sight-seeing, and that is visit its most important site, the Asklepeion, about four kilometres outside town. Discovered in 1902, it was one of the ancient world's most important shrines to the healing god Asklepios, whose followers, including Hippocrates, found that good water and fresh air and relaxing in beautiful surroundings do much to remedy the ills of body and soul.

We've learned that it's reached by a number three bus, which we assume will leave from the bus station, but when we eventually find the bus station, we realise we've assumed wrongly.

The number three actually goes from the port. We make our way through the old town and across the pretty market square and arrive at the port just in time to see the eleven-thirty bus disappearing into the distance. But we fill the time we now have on our hands usefully. We buy tickets for the twelve-thirty bus, then discover at the passenger terminal on the port that we can store our luggage safely between the time we have to leave the Pantheon tomorrow and the time our ferry for Tilos leaves in the early hours of the following day.

We spend some time in the Platanou Square, almost entirely filled by Hippocrates' plane tree. Locals claim it to be anywhere between seven hundred and two thousand years old and it's said that Hippocrates himself sat in its shade – or that of one of its predecessors – and taught his pupils. It's a massive specimen but in pretty poor shape, its huge drooping branches supported by metal scaffolding, but there's no doubting its charisma. Close by is an interesting building that was once a Turkish baths and later a salt warehouse but in recent years has been restored as a fine, if quite small, museum of Kos history.

The little bus that takes us out to the Asklepeion rattles through what appear to be country lanes and reaches its destination within about fifteen minutes. The ancient site is set on a pine-forested hillside, a series of terraces with a wide central stone staircase and stunning views across the five kilometres or so to Turkey. (Legend has it that visitors in need of a cure could stay at the Asklepeion if they sacrificed a chicken to the gods, and one guidebook warned us that we might need to do something similar to secure accommodation in Kos town. Fortunately, we didn't have any difficulty booking our room.) There's very little left to see at the Asklepeion these days, but as with most Greek archaeological sites it's the atmosphere and the sense of what once was here that makes the eight-euro admission fee well worth it. But there is an excellent little modern museum which at the very least provides some respite from the heat, now nudging the high thirties.

The old town is busy this evening and tables at the tavernas are at a premium. The Village, where we manage to find outside seats, is at the junction of two of the most popular shopping streets and so an excellent location for people-watching. The menu's slightly confusing, deliberately we suspect, but with some skilful ordering we manage to get a very good meal for twenty-seven euros. The staff all seem to be in particularly high spirits, which our waiter tells us in his near-perfect English is due to an end-of-term feeling, the nearness to the close of the season and the knowledge that they'll soon be going back to their homes and families or to university. It also helps that the television in the kitchen is showing the Greek football team beating Estonia. We're given a free ouzo each, get made to feel that we're part of the family and are treated to a bear hug from the chef when we leave.

There's live music at By Thalia, which is on the corner directly opposite our accommodation, when we get back, but it's genuine Greek music and it *is* very good. The female singer seems to be particularly popular with her audience and as I sit on our balcony it seems to give my Metaxa nightcap a little something extra.

*

This day we hadn't intended to spend in Kos town starts late. The rescheduled ferry isn't supposed to leave here until one-fifteen tomorrow morning so we're not exactly in a hurry to get going. It's almost midday by the time we've had breakfast, packed and are ready to check out of the Pantheon and we take a leisurely stroll along the damaged walkway of the seafront to the port. There we're able to store our bags at a cost of three euros each and go back on ourselves to explore the jewel in this town's crown, the ancient Agora. The Knights of St John built their town here almost a thousand years ago, but it was only in the 1930s that an earthquake revealed their market and the harbour quarter of the ancient city, a temple to Aphrodite and a fifth-century Christian basilica. It's an impressive site, apparently the first town ever to be laid out on a grid pattern.

Outside the handsome building that houses the modern municipal market we have our first drink of the day, then wander through the narrow streets of the old town again and enjoy a pita gyros and a beer in Diagora Square.

A little later, in the heat of the afternoon, we find a bench in the shade outside the cathedral of Agias Paraskevis and enjoy an ice cream from a nearby kiosk. An A4 sheet of white paper has been Blu-Tacked to the main door and is flapping in the breeze after one of its corners has become unstuck. Close inspection reveals the announcement, in spidery black felt-tip, "The church is closed due to earthquake damage". There are some serious cracks in the walls and suddenly the reason for the poor state of the seafront walkway becomes clear. A Google search for "earthquake on Kos" reminds us of what we should have remembered.

Just over a year ago, when we were in the very early stages of planning this trip, an earthquake that measured 6.6 on the Richter Scale struck in the sea just south of here. Two people were killed and more than a hundred were injured on Kos, several hundred more were injured in the Bodrum area of Turkey. The two people who died were tourists, struck by masonry when a bar collapsed, and in addition to the church outside where we are now standing, an eighteenth-century mosque in the town was also badly damaged.

Back down at sea level we have a coffee at one of the bars that are separated from the waterfront by the wide earthquake-damaged walkway and road and watch the daytrippers returning. There must be a dozen of these mock galleons with names like *Black Pearl, Captain Hook* and *Princess Dianna* (*sic*) and they're all packed to the gunwhales with happy holidaymakers, many of whom are wearing the ubiquitous coloured wristbands. They're noisy and boisterous as they disperse in all directions, heading for the parked coaches that will take them back to their hotels and an evening of pre-paid food and drink.

*

After an evening spent eating and drinking and largely killing time, we make our way back to the ferry passenger terminal at twelve-thirty, retrieve our luggage, buy a couple of coffees and sit down to wait. And wait. And wait. By one-fifteen, when the ferry should be leaving, there are forty or fifty other would-be passengers and no sign of a ship. They're all remarkably patient. The fact that a service that should have left Kos at eight in the morning has been put back by more than seventeen hours and is now running late seems not to bother them in the slightest. Some catch a little sleep, others chat as if it were the most normal thing in the world. Which it probably is.

At just after two lights appear in the distance, then become larger as what all of us hope is Hellenic Seaways' *Nissos Chios* approaches the harbour. It's almost two-thirty by the time it's loaded and pulling away again. This modern ship can apparently hold more than seventeen hundred passengers but there's probably fewer than a quarter of that number on board tonight, most of them asleep. They're sprawled lengthways on the padded benches and on the floor in the aisles. I set the alarm on my phone for a couple of hours' time, just in case the beers I've been drinking to help while away the hours should make me *too* relaxed, zip up my hoodie against the coolish air and settle down with my book.

Chapter Six

Tilos – "An unbelievable waste of money!"

It's a little after four-thirty when the *Nissos Chios* ties up in the little port of Livadia, the main settlement on the island of Tilos. We came here six years ago and immediately fell in love with the island, remote, unspoiled, tranquil and populated by a few hundred friendly, welcoming natives. We always knew we'd come back. Despite the unearthly hour, one of those friendly, welcoming natives, our landlady Katerina, is waiting for us on the quayside, a woman in her fifties who even at this time of day is immaculately dressed and made-up. It's surely above and beyond the call of duty, since we know the island, and our accommodation, Elli Bay apartments, is no more than a hundred metres along the waterfront from the point at which the ferry has docked. She shows us to our large apartment on the first floor of the complex and we fall into bed and are asleep within minutes.

By nine-thirty we're wide awake again, having our first cup of tea of the day and unpacking. Tilos, we discover when we go out to buy supplies, has changed little. Two or three minimarkets are still where they were six years ago, the square at the centre of the village – developed some years ago by an island mayor who wanted to create an 'authentic' Greek village atmosphere where none previously existed – looks remarkably familiar and all the tavernas we knew still seem to be in business. That same mayor, incidentally, a member of Greenpeace, declared the whole of the island a wildlife refuge and upset locals by banning hunting. We buy eggs and bread, wine and Metaxa and return to Elli Bay, too tired to do much other than relax on our balcony overlooking the bay and read and doze.

There's great excitement at just after six when the *Nissos Chios* appears from the direction of Rhodes. It seems like most of Livadia is down at the quayside, disembarking, embarking, greeting, waving off or just watching. The usual chaos ensues as cars, vans, taxis and minibuses manage to gridlock themselves until a port policeman – *the* port policeman, presumably – with a whistle and some flamboyant arm action tries to sort everything out. Eventually, calm is restored, and the *Nissos Chios* disappears in the direction of Nissyros, the next nearest island north, remarkably only a few minutes behind schedule.

We're in two minds where to eat this evening – Nikos in the square or Mikhailis, just behind our apartment, where six years ago we were first introduced to goat in lemon sauce. In the end the decision is taken out of our hands. Nikos is busy and Maria, the feisty, smiling, slightly larger than life New York-raised wife of the eponymous owner, is telling potential customers to come back in fifteen or twenty minutes – which on a Greek island is more likely to be forty-five minutes to an hour. Mikhailis is busy too, but it's big and they're turning things round much more quickly. We have a table within five minutes and the food and service are as good as they always were.

From what we can overhear, Tilos has become popular with the British since we were last here. Although if we've heard correctly many of them will be leaving tomorrow, it's package holiday changeover day, and this being towards the end of the season it's unlikely that the same number of newcomers will replace them. Like Lipsi, it's become one of those small Greek islands that people, particularly middle-class Brits, think they've 'discovered', that it's 'their' island. Thankfully, they're still a long way from spoiling it.

*

According to historians, six million years ago Tilos was joined to Asia Minor. When it broke away about ten thousand years ago elephants were trapped on the island and they adapted to the limited supply of food by shrinking in size down to about four feet tall. In the Charkadio Caves in the centre of the island, bones of these mini-elephants were found in the early 1970s, as well as the remains of deer and tortoises and some Stone Age pottery. Nearby, pumice cliffs and volcanic debris emanated from an eruption on Nissyros, the only volcano in the Dodecanese but dormant since the 1930s. Every weekday morning, the little bus that runs across the island, throughout the day until late in the evening, makes a detour to Charkadio, a chance to revisit some history that's too good to pass up.

The bus driver is the same small Greek man who drove us around six years ago, the bus is packed with holidaymakers heading for the beaches on the far side of the island. It's standing room only by the time we manage to squeeze ourselves on, but the fare's only a euro and it's only fifteen or twenty minutes up into the mountains so no real discomfort. The museum itself is a single large room with a variety of interesting display cases explaining that the pigmy elephants were probably hunted out of existence by man. Why bones have only been found in a single cave is a matter of conjecture, a panel on one of the cases declares, but it's possible that they were sheltering from the elements when the cave roof collapsed and trapped them.

The solitary member of staff appears to be a young man on secondment from the University of Athens and not particularly happy about being here. He gives us an excellent guided tour for two euros each but then, out of earshot of any Greeks who may have drifted in, reveals some of his grievances about his secondment – not the least being that, because of the economic situation, there's never been any electricity or mains water on the site, hence no air-conditioning, which means that at times it's like working in a sauna. Given that he probably weighs about eighteen stones, that can't be comfortable. He also explains the feature halfway down the mountain that looks like a large velodrome but is in fact a reservoir that leaks and therefore doesn't hold any of the rainwater it's supposed to store.

"An unbelievable waste of money," he says in his excellent English. "Two hundred million euros of EU subsidies to create a reservoir on an island where they have more than enough underground springs and don't need to store water. And then it leaks and just lies there dry."

Less than an hour later the bus returns to the museum to collect us and deposits us at the hillside village of Megalo Chorio ('large town'), a pretty settlement whose winding streets are barely wide enough for the bus to negotiate. There's a ruined castle at the top of the village where traces of houses dating back to the seventh century BC have been unearthed. Up a flight of stone steps there's another little museum dedicated to the mini-elephants, a tiny one-room place where we meet a delightful and very knowledgeable elderly Greek woman who explains the story of the elephants and shows us all the exhibits. She's very proud of the island, she tells us as she borrows our camera and takes our photograph in front of a glass case containing a skeleton of an elephant, and proud of the fact that so many of its young people have gone on to higher education elsewhere in Greece and to successful careers.

On the terrace at the Kastro taverna we enjoy a beer and the wonderful views from the terrace and pass the time while waiting for the bus back to Livadia with several other people who have been to the museum – including the charming Americans Bunny and Bill, whose retirement we learn comprises summers sailing around the eastern Mediterranean on one of the large yachts currently moored in Livadia and winters skiing in Aspen, Colorado. Skiing in the true sense of the word that is, although there's no doubt there's an element of Spending the Kids' Inheritance there as well. They *have* sold their apartment in Manhattan to finance their lifestyle, after all.

*

Power cuts seem to be a way of life on Tilos, and George, who runs a street corner bar and services the tables on the square, takes them in his stride. Tall, handsome, white-haired and moustachioed, he is one of the island's best known and most popular characters – and he appears to have acquired an Asian bride since we were here six years ago. She has a permanent smile and flawless English and makes George's Bar (that's its real name) even more welcoming.

We had a short power cut in Elli Bay apartments when we were getting ready to come out this evening, and now, as we sit in the square enjoying a nightcap, Livadia is plunged into darkness again. Almost before the lights go out, George is trotting across the square placing a small lantern on each of the tables, so used is he to this situation. The blackout lasts less than half an hour and, apart from the irritating alarm that has been set off at the bank, it's all good fun – and normal service has thankfully been resumed by the time we go back to Elli Bay.

*

Sunday morning and our peace is shattered by the bells at the nearby church chiming at seven-fifteen. And again at seven-thirty. And again at seven-forty-five – and so on. They are, admittedly, only short peals but the church is no more than fifty metres away and they *are* very loud. One peal sends a flock of hooded crows hurtling into the sky as if they've never heard it before and sets off a cicada in a tree next to our balcony. But it seems appropriate since we're planning to visit a monastery.

The Byzantine monastery of Saint Panteleimon is two hundred metres above the island's west coast on the slopes of Tilos's highest peak, Profitis Ilias – like every other fishing boat being named Agios Nikolaos, every highest peak on a Greek island appears to be Profitis Ilias – and every Sunday morning there's a special bus service to take tourists there. It's a hairy switchback ride up a road that is scarcely more than a rough mountain track, it's standing room only again and it has our American friend Bill cracking nervous jokes about being plunged down the mountainside. But, founded in the early fifteenth century, it *is* a beautiful spot, set in surroundings of shady cypresses and gushing streams.

The red pantile-roofed monastery is defended by a tall stone tower and contains some wonderful fifteenth-century frescoes, including one of St Panteleimon holding the monastery in his hand, and others of Paradise, and an old marble drinking fountain fringed by pots of basil. Sad that it lacks some of the serenity we normally associate with these places but that could be something to do with the coachload of Russian tourists swarming over everything.

The bus back to Livadia goes all over the island, to beaches, small villages and Megalo Chorio where, since we're thirsty, we get off and enjoy a leisurely cold beer on the terrace at Kastro, before setting off to walk the two kilometres down to the little seaside settlement of Agios Antonis. We pass a small military barracks complex and a shabby football stadium with a pristine Astroturf pitch that clearly hasn't been used for some time, we walk under a sign reading *Carpe Diem* outside a taverna called Elpidi before settling down beside the little harbour at Delfini, a fish restaurant owned and run by local fishermen.

It's good basic food but what makes it memorable is the setting, one of the most beautiful and tranquil places we've ever been, anywhere in the world. The quayside is lined with trees, sheltering us from the burning afternoon sun, the water in the little bay is choppy but an unbelievable turquoise, a handful of fishing boats bob up and down at their moorings. We're under no pressure to leave, but we eventually move to the café next door, which is almost certainly owned by the same family, and enjoy delicious ice creams before taking the late afternoon bus back to Livadia. We play a game of Spot the Goat – wondering how long it will be before they make it to the menu at Mikhailis – and in passing are lucky to catch sight of a kingfisher, unmistakable turquoise plumage glinting in the sunlight. Magical.

The wind has become even stronger by the time we go out for dinner at Sofia's, a short walk from Elli Bay along the waterfront walkway. Vasilis, son of the eponymous Sofia, has drawn down the transparent plastic screens and for the first time since we've been on the island we eat inside. But it gives us the chance to admire his collection of football scarves which cover every square centimetre of the taverna's walls and ceiling.

"I used to have a Manchester United scarf behind the bar because George Best was my hero," Vasilis tells us. "People just kept bringing others in for me and when they came back they expect to see them up on the walls."

It's an impressive collection, the usual suspects such as Arsenal, Real Madrid, Juventus and so on, plus a fair number of smaller, and occasionally non-league, clubs from all over the world. And as we try and spot ones we recognise we have the inevitable power cut. Vasilis copes magnificently, bringing small oil lamps to everyone's table seconds after the lights have gone out. We may not be able to see our food very well, but through the plastic curtain we're treated to the sight of a wonderful star-filled sky. I was going to suggest that they should have power cuts more often, such is the beauty they reveal, but however much the islanders seem to take them in their stride, it can't really be fun.

*

"Sooner or later, they say you find *your* Greek island," the loud middle-aged Yorkshireman who's on holiday on his own tells the two women who he has just sat down beside. "I've found mine," he adds, with an expansive wave of his arm. We're sitting outside the Mikro café on the water's edge enjoying a pre-lunch drink, fortunately a couple of tables away – close enough to hear everything he says but too far to be drawn into the conversation. He's from Sheffield, we learn, and will tell his life story to anyone who's prepared to listen. Or too polite to get up and walk away. We have to feel a little sorry for him. By his own admission he'll talk to anyone when he's on holiday but to no one when he's at home. At work he simply gets his head down, disturbs no one and hopes no one will disturb him. But when he comes to the islands, he becomes a different person.

From what we can gather, he'd met these two women, a mother and daughter, in the square yesterday evening after he'd already had several drinks, and he apologises for what he believes was inappropriate behaviour. They don't seem concerned or are just being polite. When they get up to go to the beach, he offers one last piece of advice. "Don't stand at the back of the ferry when you're leaving the island," he says. "Don't look back or you'll never return."

We pay our bill and quickly move on to the Nautilos (*sic*) taverna a couple of doors away. There's a table occupied by a group of Scandinavians, most of whom appear to be over sixty. The waiter/manager takes a shine to one of the women, standing behind her chair and singing two or three what appear to be Greek love songs. When he's finished, he flamboyantly kisses her hand. "It will be five euros more next time," he says. "For the singing."

By nine this evening, the *Panagia Spiniali*, the little ferry that seems to do two journeys to Rhodes and back every Wednesday, has brought dozens more holidaymakers to Livadia, but the ever-smiling Maria still manages to find us a table at Nikos. She manages to be both bossy and warm-hearted at the same time, chiding diners for not finishing their meals then embracing them enthusiastically and giving them a souvenir bookmark when they leave. She has the kind of personality that could only have been developed in New York. Nikos's rabbit stifado is delicious and we fall into conversation with a couple of late-middle-aged sisters on the next table – which is unavoidable since the tables are squeezed so tightly together.

They're an interesting pair, born in a village in the far north of Scotland where one of them still lives and retains her soft Scottish accent. The other has lived in London for many years and when she speaks gives no hint as to where she may have been born. She has travelled a great deal, all over the world, while her sister has spent her entire life, apart from holidays like this, in their village near Wick. But they're equally interested in what we've been doing and wish us well on the final leg of our journey as they leave.

On the table on the other side two young men have been seated by Maria, and after they've ordered their food there's a long and animated conversation between the three of them. Without prompting, they all turn to face us and explain in English what they've been talking about. During the conversation, Maria and one of the young men have realised that they're cousins, or possibly second cousins.

"My grandfather was from Tilos," the young man explains. "He moved to Rhodos many years ago. I grew up there and this is the first time I've been to Tilos."

"My father went to America when I was just a baby," Maria adds. "He lost touch with some of his family here. I don't know how many cousins I have in the islands, but now I have one more than I thought."

*

As we sit on our balcony enjoying a last breakfast on Tilos, we hear the familiar reassuring sound of the time signal pips on Radio Four. In the garden of the neighbouring property a man is listening to the *Today* programme on his iPad. The *Dodekanisos Express* service to Rhodes doesn't leave Livadia until four-thirty, so we have almost an entire day to spend just soaking up the sun and the atmosphere on this island that we've loved just as much as when we were first here.

Katerina lets us leave our bags in her reception area at Elli Bay and we walk into the square, settle down outside Paulos, a little café we've never tried before, and spend an interesting hour or so people-watching. There's a little cloud around but it's still a very warm and pleasant day, only slightly spoiled by a group of seven or eight very loud and excitable Finns on a day trip from Rhodes. An expensive day trip at that. There are no cheap excursions here and our single tickets alone have cost twenty-seven euros each.

We have a final Tilos lunch at Mikhailis, much quieter than usual so the service is even better, then linger on a bench on the seafront to absorb the magic of this little island for the last time (on this trip, at least). There's still a breeze, though the wind is nowhere near as strong as it had been a couple of days ago and we're not anticipating an uncomfortable journey to Rhodes. And then we collect our bags from the Elli Bay reception, receive a farewell hug from the ever-charming Katerina, and take the five-minute walk to the port to join the scattering of travellers awaiting the sixteen-thirty service to Rhodes.

Chapter Seven

Rhodes – The end of the line

We've ignored the Yorkshireman's advice and have been standing outside at the stern of the *Dodekanisos Express*, watching as the little island of Tilos has disappeared into the distance, and now we're reversing into the pretty harbour of the even smaller island of Chalki. It's like a miniature version of Symi, topped with a Disney castle on a pointed hill, home to around three hundred locals and somewhere we'd considered staying for a few days if only it had been better served by the ferries and there had been more tourist accommodation. We linger a few minutes while several crates are unloaded and two people come aboard, then pull out of the harbour and continue on to Rhodes, spending the remainder of the journey in the crowded and chilly, over-air-conditioned passenger lounge.

We sail into Rhodes Town at around six-thirty on a beautiful evening, into a port that is sadly dominated by four monstrous cruise ships, one of which we later discover carries over three thousand passengers and almost as many crew. But it's the time of day when, hopefully, they're about to leave. Perched on the island's northern tip, Rhodes Town is the capital of the Dodecanese and by far the archipelago's largest settlement, home to almost two-thirds of Rhodes's population. It's split neatly between Old and New Towns, and we make our way past the massive walls of the former to find our hotel in the latter, a maze of streets lined with brightly lit designer shops. We've booked a room at the Hotel Moschos, which we find in a busy side street in the heart of the shopping district. It's a bright noisy location and right under the flight path into the airport. Perhaps it will be quieter later.

As the evening falls, we sit outside a café on Eleftherias, opposite the Mandraki Harbour. A short distance to our left is the lighthouse and the fort of Agios Nikolaos, built in the fifteenth century to defend the harbour from Turkish attacks, and a bronze stag and doe marking where the fabled Colossus may have stood. When the Knights Hospitallers of Saint John settled on the island after the Crusades, a chain spanned the harbour's entrance, and every ship that came in had to pay a two per cent tax on the value of its cargo to help fund the war effort.

Large ferries, cruise ships and other cargo-carrying craft now use the Commercial Harbour, and Mandraki is full of small ferry boats, yachts and the ubiquitous excursion boats. Theirs is a sophisticated business these days. The skippers no longer stand by their boats all evening selling tickets for tomorrow's excursion. Non-stop gaudy neon displays scroll details of the trips, times and costs, with information on how to book by phone or online.

As we sit and enjoy our drinks, the sky blackens, and in the distance we hear several loud cracks of thunder. A fierce electric storm seems to be raging over the Turkish mainland, lighting the sky like some massive fireworks display. It continues for much of the evening without coming any closer and unaccompanied, it would seem, by rain. Surprisingly, by nine o'clock many of the tavernas along the harbour are either closing or already closed. Their trade seems largely to be the cruise ship passengers and by this time in the evening they've had enough. We eventually find a rather shabby establishment next to the castle walls and just outside the market serving basic, but very good, Greek food.

And when we make our way back to the Hotel Moschos we can see that the storm has abated – even if, at almost midnight, flights are still coming into the airport. So maybe not such a quiet night after all.

*

We're awake early, around seven, and it's noisy, but it's only to be expected in a town of this size. The planes seem to have stopped but they have been replaced by traffic in the street below our second-floor window, drivers impatiently honking their horns if they're held up for more than a few seconds. Refuse trucks and buses trying to thread their way between carelessly parked cars. People shouting at friends on the other side of the street. This is a busy working town in Greece.

There's one thing every visitor to Rhodes must do and that is visit the Old Town, a Unesco World Heritage Site, and after breakfast we're on our way. It's early for us but we're by no means the first visitors. Another three massive cruise ships have moored overnight in the Commercial Harbour and as we pass through the massive medieval walls via the d'Amboise Gate it's already teeming with wrist-banded tourists and tour guides carrying a variety of objects above their heads so they don't lose their charges. Many of the tourists are drawn to the souvenir sellers and caricature artists in the square just inside the gate. We walk a little further to the inner sanctum, the Collachium, where, at the highest point in the Old Town, stands the castle within a castle, the Palace of the Grand Masters.

We pay our seven euros each (seniors' concessions) to enter a fourteenth-century citadel which was modelled on the Popes' Palace in Avignon. Many of the Grand Masters on Rhodes were French and French was the official language of the Order and the island. The Turks used the palace as a prison, even after a great explosion in the middle of the nineteenth century when the floor collapsed, and before the Second World War the Italians did the same until Mussolini ordered that the palace be reconstructed as his summer residence. They brought in floor mosaics from Kos, installed a lift and modern plumbing, but unfortunately for Il Duce the war broke out and he was unable to enjoy the palace's hundred and fifty-eight rooms. No more than a tenth of the rooms are open to the public today, but we're impressed by a huge marble coat of arms above one of the fireplaces declaring that it was restored by the King-Emperor Victor Emanuel III in 1939 and by the permanent exhibitions dedicated to Rhodes's history.

Outside the Old Town walls we find the Nea Aghora, the New Market, no longer home to the greengrocers, butchers and fishmongers of Rhodes but to a collection of fast-food stands and tavernas, outside of which the touts work desperately to attract business in what is now the tail end of the holiday season. I buy today's *Times* (my first since Kos) and we settle down to enjoy a final authentic pita gyros. (You can get them in Brighton these days, from a mobile kitchen in the city centre, but they're about three times the price and nowhere near as good.) And then we do something we've thought about doing in towns and cities all over Europe but never quite made it – we take a sightseeing tour on one of those little road trains that looks like it belongs in a children's amusement park.

It costs us seven euros each and proves to be one of the best investments we've made since we've been in Greece. We skirt around the Old Town walls to the ancient acropolis of Rhodes, the wonderfully named Monte Smith (after Admiral Sydney Smith, apparently), past the ruins of the Asklepeion and the Cave of the Nymphs to the partly-restored second-century-BC Temple of Apollo and the ancient Stadium. And then on to the broad seafront road and past rows of smart beachfront hotels with swimming pools and sun terraces that mean their guests don't have to cross the road to go to the beach. The seven-star Rhodos Park and the Grand Summer Astir Palace are supposedly among the most luxurious hotels in the world, although while filming *Pole to Pole* Michael Palin stayed in Rhodes Town and plumped for the considerably more modest Cavo d'Oro, in a restored thirteenth-century house near the Commercial Harbour, and was more than pleased with his accommodation.

And then, all too soon, we're back where we started, outside the main Post Office and close to the Evangelismos cathedral and the sixteenth-century Murad Reis mosque, set off by a minaret reconstructed more recently, surprisingly, by the Greek government. It's been a wonderful informative and entertaining tour, if not the most comfortable, and we've seen more of and learned more about Rhodes than we might have under our own steam.

*

There's a point at the end of every trip, no matter how memorable it's been, how long it's been, how far away from home you may be, that you wish you were Captain James T Kirk and you could say, "Beam me up, Scotty." Today is one of those occasions. This has been one of the most wonderful, unforgettable experiences, but there's a sort of empty feeling in my stomach as I complete our packing at just after seven in the morning and contemplate the journey ahead. Once you get to this point, you just want to be home – or, at least, I do. You want to see the children and grandchildren. You want to enjoy a pint of Harvey's with your friends. You want to be able to go to the corner shop for your morning newspaper. The ten-hour journey ahead doesn't seem that inviting. We have the breakfast that's included in the price of our room at the Moschos then wheel our bags the short distance to the bus stop just outside the New Market. There's a bus waiting with the word "Airport," in English, and a picture of a plane on the front, but that doesn't stop two elderly men who are sitting outside a café from trying to help us.

"Where do you want?" one of them asks.

I don't like to be rude, so I answer, "Airport," raising my tone on the second syllable so it sounds a little like a question.

"That one," the old boy replies, indicating the only bus in sight. We'll miss such thoughtfulness, the real kindness of strangers.

"Thanks."

Diagoras International Airport, the fourth busiest in Greece, is about fifteen kilometres from Rhodes Town, the fare is two euros sixty each and the journey takes less than half an hour. Diagoras is Rhodes's national hero, a Greek boxer from the fifth century BC, a large statue of whom we have seen at a busy junction on our road train tour yesterday. One of the large Blue Star Ferries ships we spotted in the Commercial Harbour is named *Diagoras*. The local football team is Diagoras FC and bars and tavernas all over the island bear his name. He was an Olympic champion, as well as having won multiple victories at the Isthmian, Nemean and Pythian Games. He is truly revered.

We hadn't known how long the bus journey would take and as a result we're at the airport far too early for our twelve-twenty flight. But we're able to check in and drop our bags and are told the flight is on time. It's a smart modern airport with a large duty-free shop and a good selection of food outlets – although the longest queues are inevitably outside Burger King and Starbucks. We browse the shops then buy a couple of coffees and settle down with our books. Since I can't get along with e-readers, for this trip I adopted my sister's routine with books. You pack your suitcase first, then weigh it. Then you add the books you want to take until you reach the airline's weight limit. Unlike the American writer Cheryl Strayed, whose *Wild*, the account of her trek on the Pacific Crest Trail, is one of the books I've just finished reading, I do not tear out the pages I've read each evening and burn them in order to lighten my load.

It's about an hour later when our flight's details first appear on the information board – followed by "Delayed 13.45," almost an hour and a half late. It's an opportunity for a final, unexpected Greek meal, an excellent slice of moussaka and a small bottle of red wine, in the self-service restaurant before we make our way to the departure gate when the word "Boarding" eventually appears. Despite the length of time we've been away and the desire to get home as quickly as possible, an extra two hours in a Greek airport, which is what it turns out to be before we board, doesn't seem so bad after all. Even the airports, particularly the provincial ones, have a uniquely Greek atmosphere, something that lifts them above the usual faceless, stateless we-could-be-anywhere atmosphere that pervades most of the world's air terminals.

On board our easyJet flight to Gatwick, the captain apologises for the delay. We hadn't been misled when we checked in, the flight had indeed been on time when it left the UK. But somewhere between Gatwick and Greece one of the passengers had suffered what appeared to be a heart attack, the pilot tells us, and the flight had been diverted to Thessaloniki so the patient could receive hospital treatment. A spontaneous round of applause breaks out among the passengers when the captain describes his crew as heroes for the way they handled the emergency.

We can feel the change in temperature as we wait for our

bags to appear on the carousel in the baggage reclaim area at Gatwick and are glad that we've both put a sweater in our hand luggage. As we wait for a train to Brighton it's cold, windy and it begins to rain. We've had rain while we've been away – but at least it was warm rain!

Yasou Greece.